THE
PICTURE
FRAMING
COURSE

THE
PICTURE
FRAMING
COURSE

Pete Bingham

STACKPOLE
BOOKS

Copyright © 1995 by Merehurst Ltd.
First Published 1995 by Merehurst Ltd., Great Britain

Published 1997 by
STACKPOLE BOOKS
5067 Ritter Road
Mechanicsburg, PA 17055

Printed in Singapore

10   9   8   7   6   5   4   3   2   1

FIRST U.S. EDITION

Color separation by Global Colour, Malaysia
Design by Watermark Communications

Photography:
Mark Gatehouse, 10–30, 34–39, 41–43, 46–49, 52–53, 62–65, 82–83, 116–117
Lu Jeffrey, with styling by Kate Hardy, 5, 87, 91, 95, 99, 103, 107, 111, 115
Philip Ward, all other step-by-step photos

Library of Congress Cataloging-in-Publication

Bingham, Pete.
    The picture framing course / Pete Bingham.—1st. U.S. ed.
        p.   cm.
    Includes index.
    0-8117-1246-X
    1. Picture frames and framing. I. Title.
N8550.B464   1997   97-10857
749'.7—dc21   CIP

Contents

Introduction

A picture frame performs an extremely useful function: it protects the picture from dust and moisture and provides a simple way of hanging it on the wall.

But there's a lot more to picture framing than that. A well-chosen – and well-executed – picture frame, together with the right mount and the right decorative treatment, can enhance a picture in much the same way that a good pianist can bring out the best in Beethoven and a good actor can bring Shakespeare to life.

Subtlety is the watchword and the framer must use tasteful restraint in the execution of his craft and strive to pick up the mood and style of the subject in question. But it is important not to go 'over the top' and let the frame overpower the picture. As a picture framer for more than 30 years, one thing I have learnt is that if a client says "Oh, what a beautiful frame", I have failed: the picture should be seen first and the frame and the picture should complement one another so that they appear as a complete entity, with neither outshining the other.

This book introduces you to the art of picture framing and also lets you into the secrets of the picture framer's practical skills.

Early beginnings

Picture framing is one of the oldest crafts known to man, almost pre-dating documented history. Apart from the obvious purpose of containing a picture neatly or protecting it, the creative ideas of early artisans soon began to make themselves felt and plain wood mouldings began to appear with decorations, usually by carving in the wood. It later became obvious that some pictures or other objects needed to be kept away from the glass to prevent damage from condensation on the inside of the glass. The mount was invented for just that purpose: a simple piece of cardboard with an aperture cut in it, the mount quickly evolved into an inherent part of the framed presentation, carrying decorations of all types.

It was not long before plain cardboard gave way to specially designed board in an increasingly wide range of colours. At this point, picture framing became a craft in its own right, although up to about 200 years ago, it was often an adjunct to another closely related craft such as joinery. Interestingly, much early picture framing was performed by coffin-makers – presumably because they possessed the appropriate tools and access to the raw materials.

By around the end of the 18th century, however, picture framing began to emerge as a specific occupation – often with the proud job description 'Picture Framers, Carvers and Gilders', giving a good idea of what a framer was generally expected to do. Today, of course, picture framing is a specialised craft of its own.

Modern developments

The single factor which has turned picture framing into a specialised craft was the development of dedicated machinery and equipment. This happened mainly from the early part of this century when machines for mitring picture frame moulding first began to appear. Mount-cutting machines followed some time after that, but the proliferation of all the types of framing equipment to which a modern framer has access has only really happened in the past 25 to 30 years.

The choice of timber mouldings used for picture framing has developed over a much longer period but again, the enormous choice now available from manufacturers is a recent development.

The home picture framer can get involved at almost any level from buying ready-made frames and mounts and merely inserting his or her own pictures to going the whole hog and making the frames and cutting the mounts from the raw materials.

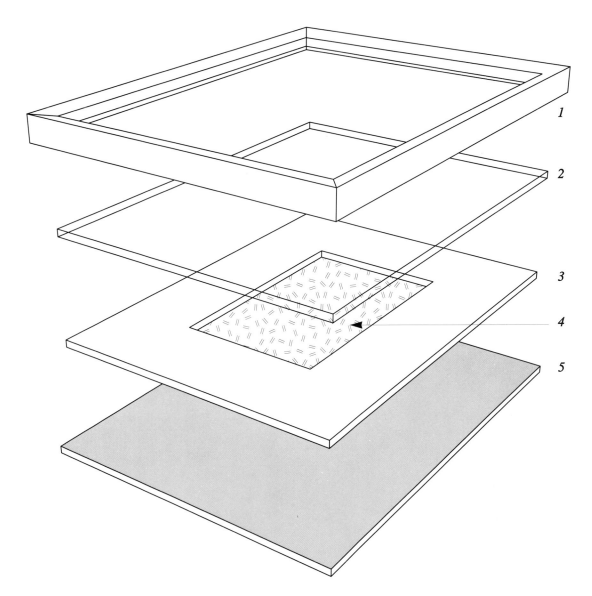

The picture framing sandwich

Most picture frames consist of five separate components joined together. In front of the picture itself is a surrounding mount with a rectangular 'window' cut out of it plus a sheet of glass; behind it is a backing board; and surrounding the whole thing is a rectangular frame, made usually out of wood.

The elements of the picture framing 'sandwich':
1. Frame
2. Glass
3. Mount-board
4. Picture
5. Backing

Not every frame is like this, of course – oil paintings, for example, are never framed with glass in front; some pictures have no surrounding mount (known as 'close' framing); some may have an oval, circular or other shape of 'window' in the mount and some may have a hexagonal or octagonal frame.

But this variation is part of the magic of picture framing: there is no 'right' way to frame any particular picture – the framing is a personal expression of how you feel about the picture in question. Both the mount and the frame can be decorated in a number of ways to enhance the overall effect, allowing you to put your own individual 'stamp' on the final result.

Order of working

Most amateur picture framers, particularly those just starting off, will not want to cut their own glass. It takes a lot of space to store and to cut glass and, once cut, glass cannot be made any bigger and cutting a tiny amount off a piece of glass is not easy. A better answer is to take the finished frame to a glass merchant for the glass to be cut to the correct size. The order of working is then:

1. Cut (and perhaps decorate) the mount
2. Secure the picture to the mount
3. Cut the backing to the same size as the mount
4. Make the frame (and perhaps decorate it) to suit the size of the mount/backing
5. Check the fit of mount and backing in the frame and buy the glass, pre-cut to the same size
6. Clean the glass and assemble glass, mount, picture and backing as a taped 'sandwich'
7. Place the sandwich in the frame and seal with tape
8. Fit the hooks or hanging wire.

If you are able to cut your own glass, the order is modified slightly with the glass being cut early on (after the mount is cut) and the frame being made after the 'sandwich' has been assembled. This is the method I use and I find it makes for ease of handling and helps to keep the glass and picture clean.

When making more than one frame (for a set of matching pictures or prints, say), you can adapt the working order to a 'production line' method – for example, cutting all the mouldings in one go.

Quality, neatness and cleanliness are paramount in framing. The finished job should look just as good at the back as it does at the front – it is surprising how many people will immediately turn the frame round and look at the back. If you want a professional job, be meticulous in finishing off the frame. Make sure all sharp corners are sanded, any gaps filled, all glass cleaned and all bits of unsightly dirt removed.

Amateur or professional?

This book has been written for the serious amateur framer – the kind of person who is interested enough to go to evening classes and who is prepared to spend the equivalent of a week's wages on buying equipment. But some 'amateurs' are inspired by early success to take it up professionally – even if only on a part-time basis. This can mean a considerable further investment (perhaps many weeks' income) in the accurate and labour-saving machinery which professional picture framers use and the provision of a dedicated space for both the storage of materials and the making, decoration and assembly of frames. But I can assure you it will give hours of pleasure and satisfaction.

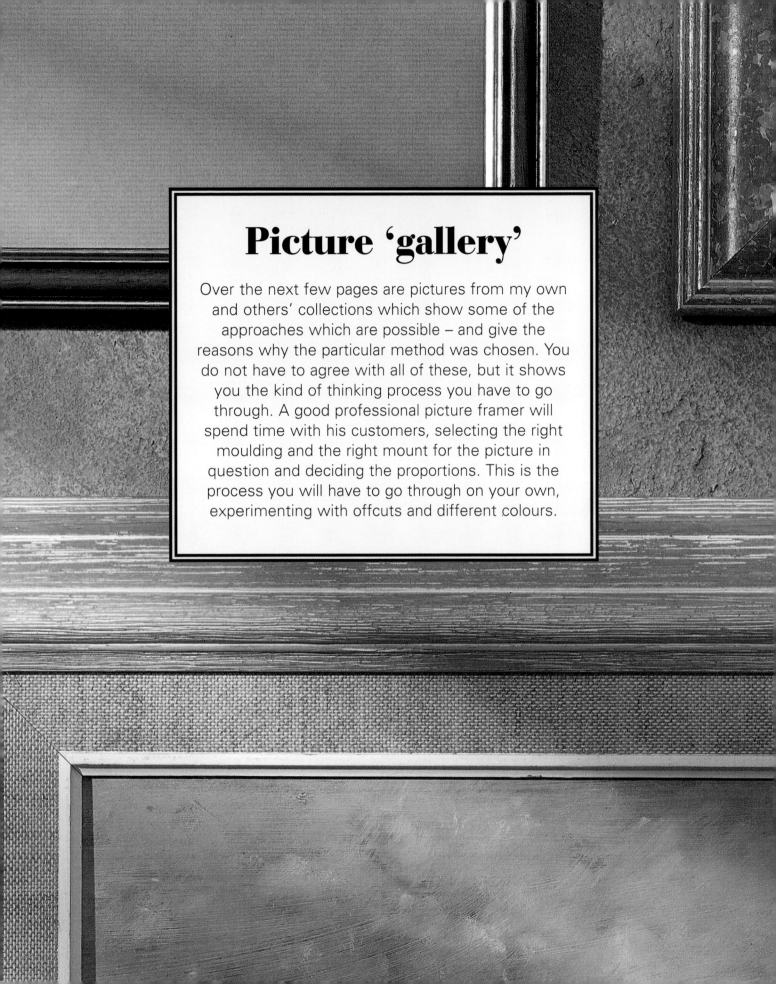

Picture 'gallery'

Over the next few pages are pictures from my own and others' collections which show some of the approaches which are possible – and give the reasons why the particular method was chosen. You do not have to agree with all of these, but it shows you the kind of thinking process you have to go through. A good professional picture framer will spend time with his customers, selecting the right moulding and the right mount for the picture in question and deciding the proportions. This is the process you will have to go through on your own, experimenting with offcuts and different colours.

Picture 'gallery'

An oil painting of a beach scene framed in lightly stained pine to give a 'sand' effect surround. The wooden beaded 'slip' is actually a second moulding positioned inside the main moulding – and, as with all oil paintings, no mount or glass has been used.

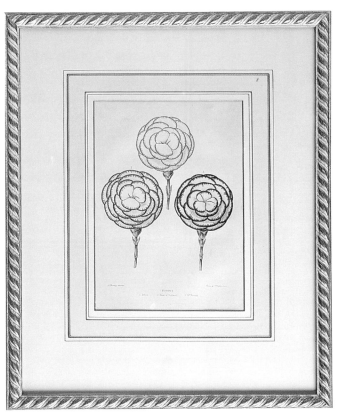

An old black-and-white print is enhanced with a black-core light-blue/grey mount to add interest. The modern marbled black-and-white moulding is a surprising – but effective – choice.

This flower print has been given a subtle treatment with the barest of washlines and green and red ink-lines echoing the flower colours. A gilded bevel and a gold cream rope-effect moulding complete the elegant effect.

Fred the ginger tomcat comes from a calendar – but 'close' framing (without a mount) in a fine maple wood moulding gives the illusion that he is an original oil painting.

Highly coloured photographs can be difficult to frame. The colour chosen for this mount tones with the bright blouse in the photograph, whilst the ornate gold moulding balances the sumptuous colours. The oval aperture is a traditional (and attractive) way of presenting a single subject portrait.

A traditional wide moulding has been given a complementary hand-painted dragged effect by the artist of this oil painting.

An example of a multi-aperture mount. A lightly textured mount-board has been chosen for this fabric collage, whilst the understated dark moulding give the lace figures added prominence.

This mount was cut specifically to follow the lines of the picture – it incorporates a rectangle, a circle and an oval. The moulding has been stained to match the colours in the flowers.

A rustic treatment for a rustic scene with a wooden mount and frame to match the atmosphere of the painting. The bare wood of the moulding is intended to give a 'looking through the pigsty door' effect.

A lavish treatment for a botanical print. A buff-coloured mount was given a green inner wash (including the bevel) which in turn is surrounded with a wide ribbon of marbled paper edged in gold. A fine black spatter 'ages' the moulding.

This watercolour has been given a double mount as an alternative to the traditional washline (see the project on page 104); the inner mount needs to be lighter than the outer one so that the eye is drawn into the picture. A silver moulding was chosen to complement the delicate cool colours in the picture.

A suitable Art Nouveau frame, plus depth and decoration provided by two slips, gives this Holman Hunt print a lift from its dark and sinister content.

Classic 'grand' treatment of a
Victorian landscape oil painting
with a wide, sculptured and
gilded frame.

This miniature picture has been
treated as a jewel. Setting it in a
gold mount, with a decorative slip
inside an over-large moulding,
makes it look tiny and precious.
The concave face of the moulding
helps to draw the eye in to
the picture.

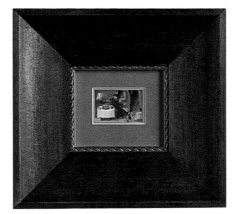

The use of a gilded wooden slip
inside the mount aperture creates
the impression of a very wide frame
moulding. On this old butterfly
print the inner slip is plain whilst
the outer gilt moulding is highly
decorated – a more decorative slip
would be matched with a plainer
outer moulding. A plain mount
between the two is all that
is needed.

This treatment shows what you can do with a simple postcard! The black-and-white photograph has been given prominence by its wide plain mount, surrounded by a unobtrusive narrow black moulding – a typical 1930s treatment. The black-core bevel gives the impression that the photograph is set deeper into the mount.

The large amount of white space forming the background to this decorative stencil means that it can be framed without a mount. Sponging softens the colour of the moulding.

Round plates present an interesting framing challenge. In this example, the plate is set in plain white foamcore and set in a hexagonal frame made from flat wooden moulding.

A bird's-eye maple frame with a gold 'sight edge' plus an opulent velvet mount provides the intended 'drawing-room' look to this Victorian print.

An alternative treatment for a black-and-white print – with no mount and all the decoration being done on the moulding. For this French architectural print, the moulding has been hand painted in black and cream, with fleur-de-lis motifs painted in at the corners as a reminder of its origins.

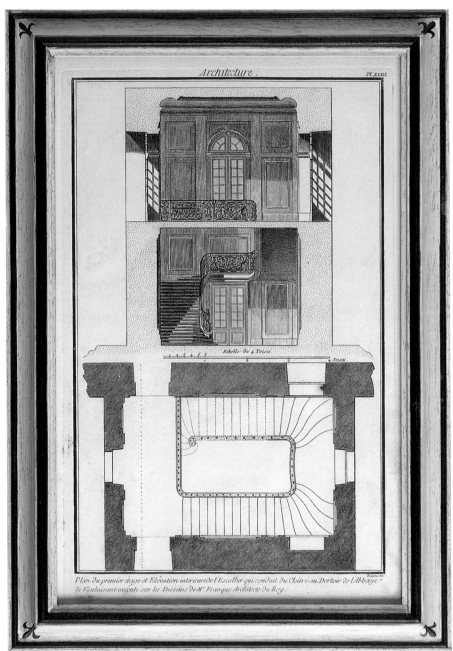

Calligraphy needs a treatment which will not detract from its message. Here, a plain triple mount all in the same light cream colour leads the eye into the verse, whilst an antique maple frame matches the age of the writing. Fussily decorated mounts clash horribly with calligraphy.

A fruit print, given an 'antiqued' treatment with a verdigris crackle glaze. The gold mount has been muted by sponging in a colour to match the frame and prevent it appearing too bright.

This oil painting (of well-known TV characters) has been given a feeling of depth by the use of a wooden surround and a linen slip within the frame. The wooden surround has been coated with textured paint and coloured to indicate the local natural stone and the whole is finished off with a jolly washed pine frame.

A colourful crayon drawing like this can have a plain mount as no further decoration is needed. It can also take a modern metal frame, picking up one of the minor colours in the picture – using one of the main colours would make the frame compete with the drawing.

A rich treatment of a classical scene. The blue-clouded mount has been given a slightly deeper blue washline (picking out the delicate blues in the picture), a double gold line with a bronzed marbled strip and is finished off with a gilded inner bevel. Note the understated wooden frame, lightly brushed with gold.

An example of 'close' framing (no mount). The hand-painted navy moulding, spattered in gold, picks up the blue of the cups. Note the gilded inner slip effect achieved by painting the inner edge of the moulding in gold.

A light-hearted treatment. This print of a coot is framed in a plain wooden moulding hand–painted with a 'chequerboard' effect in keeping with its simple country style. A simple grey washline edged in black picks out the grey/black of the feathers.

The subtle colour choice of a grey/terracotta double mount for this theatrical dance costume design complements the colours in the costume. The elegant treatment is finished off with a sophisticated black and gold moulding.

Equipment & materials

To start with, you can carry out your own picture framing at home with a minimum amount of specialist equipment – much of the work can be done with tools and equipment you may well already own. As you move on in picture framing, and demand higher standards, you will want to buy more and more specialised tools and equipment – to achieve more accurate and more attractive results. Always buy the best quality tools and equipment you can afford: cheap goods are a false economy.

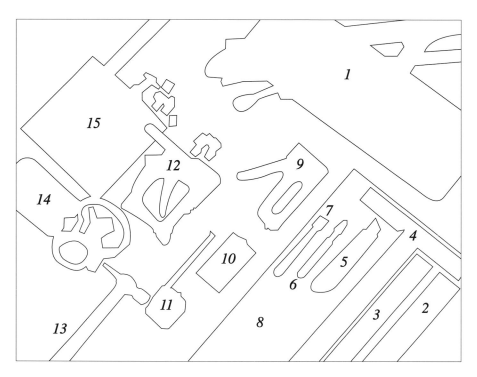

The main tools and equipment you need to make a start in picture framing.

1. Mitre saw
2. Metal straight-edge
3. Plastic rule
4. Graduated T-square
5. Trimming knife
6. Ruling pen
7. Oil-filled glass cutter
8. Cutting mat
9. Staple gun
10. Hand-held mount cutter
11. Steel tape measure
12. Glazier's gun and darts
13. Hammer
14. Picture framing clamp
15. Hand-operated underpinner

Main tools and equipment

To frame a picture you will need tools and equipment to cut the moulding, to assemble the cut pieces to make the frame, to cut the mount, to cut the backing board (and, perhaps, the glass) and to assemble the frame. You may also need the wherewithal to decorate both the frame and the mount and to carry out any necessary finishing of the final frame.

Cutting the moulding

The basic requirement for any rectangular picture frame is to 'mitre' the moulding at an angle of exactly 45° – that is, half a right angle. Two mouldings cut at this angle will join together to form a perfect corner.

So the most important practical piece of equipment for any framer is the mitring device, the most basic of which is the **mitre block** – a simple 'L'-shaped piece of hardwood or plastic with slots cut in it to guide the blade of a tenon saw at angles of both 45° and 90°. Whilst this piece of equipment is a boon to the amateur home carpenter cutting mitres for something like fitting architrave moulding around door frames, it is really too rough and ready to provide the good mitres needed for picture framing.

Better is the U-shaped **mitre**

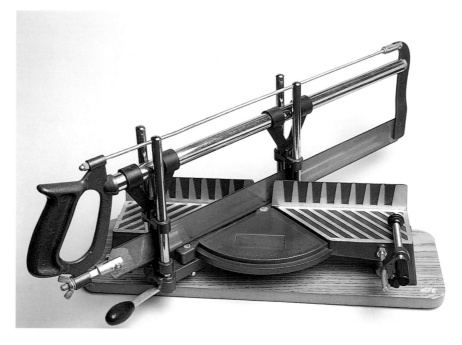

Hand-operated mitre saw fitted with moulding clamp.

box, which has the advantage that it supports both ends of the saw. It, too, has slots at 45° and 90° and the more expensive mitre boxes have metal guides to protect the slots, which can soon wear out in an all-wooden box.

A third choice for use with your own tenon saw is the **corner clamp**. This is mainly used for frame joining, but the more expensive clamps have a guide slot across the corner for cutting mitres.

For anything other than occasional picture frames, however, the best mitring tool for the amateur is the hand-operated **mitre saw** (shown in the photo above). Made from metal, and with its own fine-toothed saw blade, this machine allows you to cut not just 45° and 90° angles, but also the angles necessary for multi-sided frames – 60° for hexagonal and 67½° for octagonal frames. The moulding sits on a flat metal base and the saw blade is locked at the required angle, allowing you to make the cut. A mitre saw gives a very accurate result and is widely used by professionals – especially for some gilded or highly decorated mouldings which could be damaged by the professional guillotine cutter. A mitre saw is comparatively inexpensive and will give many years of reliable and accurate service; most designs have a 'stop' to allow two or more pieces to be cut to exactly the same length and some have a clamp to secure the moulding.

Frame joining

Having achieved four well-mitred pieces of moulding, the next requirement is to fasten them together effectively. The simplest method is to stick them together with PVA wood adhesive, using a clamp to hold them while the adhesive dries.

There are several types of clamp you can use for picture framing. The simplest is a **string clamp**, where four pre-shaped plastic corner blocks are held by a terylene cord which is locked by a plastic cleat. A wider **tape clamp** gives a more positive action, but better than either of these is a purpose-made **picture framing clamp** which has three angled corner pieces (the body of the clamp forming the fourth) and a ratchet tightening handle to pull the tape tight around all four corners. A simple quick-release mechanism allows the clamp to be removed and extra corner pieces (supplied) can be used for multi-sided frames.

A purpose-made picture framing clamp can be used for rectangular or multi-sided frames.

A metal **corner clamp** holds two lengths of moulding exactly at right angles, but does not press them together – and to join a frame in this way means having four such clamps or waiting in turn while the adhesive at each corner dries!

Adhesive alone is not usually enough as the only method of fastening a corner. To be doubly sure, the addition of some other form of strengthening is required, usually a veneer pin driven in from the outside of the corner with a hammer: a corner clamp is helpful to hold each corner square and secure when doing this. A hand-held or electric drill is needed to make a pilot hole for the pin – I find it best to use a headless pin in the drill chuck to do this as tiny drill bits tend either to break or to get lost.

To achieve more professional corners, you can use a machine called an **underpinner**. This is a clever device which drives a 'W' shaped metal wedge into the moulding from the back, across the mitre line at the corner. One, two or three wedges may be used depending on the width of frame moulding. Underpinning gives a very strong corner (a smear of PVA wood adhesive is used as well) and has the advantage of being very quick. Professionals will use a foot-operated, floor-standing,

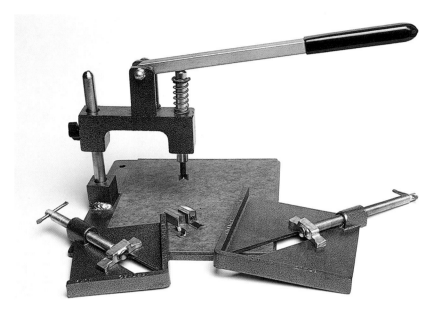

underpinner, but for the amateur a bench-mounted, hand-operated, underpinner is more than adequate. Normally, this comes with a choice of different sizes of corner vice for holding two pieces of moulding square.

A bench-mounted, hand-operated underpinner with frame-holding corner vices and wedges.

Metal corner clamp with slots for cutting mitres.

Mount cutting

To cut a mount (or backing board) to size, all that is needed is a metal straight-edge and a trimming knife of the 'Stanley' type. Choose a good, heavy, metal straight-edge with a bevel (which you will need when decorating a mount), preferably at least 1.2m (48in) long and graduated, to cut down marking-out time. For safety's sake, go for the type of trimming knife which has a retractable blade. A large self-healing cutting mat is a suitable surface to rest the mount-board on while cutting it to shape.

The main work with mount cutting, however, is to cut an aperture in the mount-board to form a 'window' around the picture. Cutting a straight-sided aperture is not difficult with the trimming knife, but a bevelled edge (leading the eye into the picture) looks infinitely better and reveals the white (or, sometimes, black or coloured) core of the mount-board as an added decorative effect. Bevelled edges are not easy to cut accurately by hand with a trimming knife and straight-edge (though it can be done); the tool to use is a **hand-held mount cutter**. This is a small, comfortably shaped, alloy or plastic tool with a replaceable cutting blade held in it at the correct angle (45°) and it is run along the side of a metal straight-

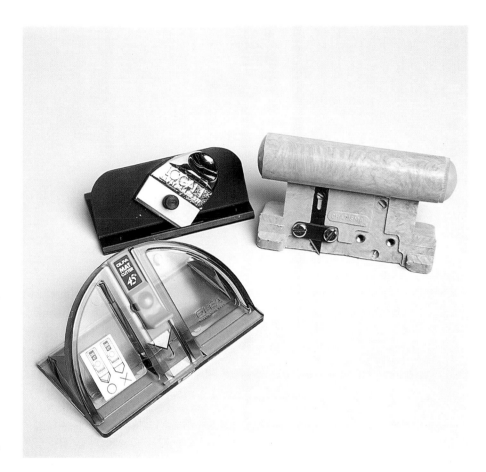

edge. With most hand-held mount cutters, the straight-edge can be positioned on the cutting line rather than away from it. A spare piece of mount-board (not a self-healing mat) should be used under the mount being cut. An artist's scalpel or a razor blade is a useful tool for cleaning out the corners of the window. For standard sizes of picture, you can buy pre-cut mount-board with the bevelled window already cut for you (including oval shapes).

Hand-held mount cutters are relatively inexpensive and make a perfect 45° bevel.

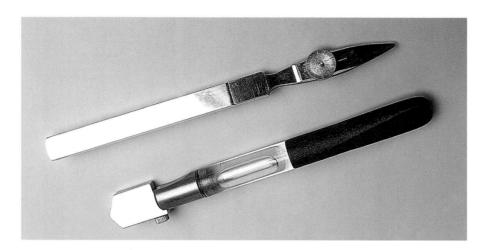

Two essential picture-framing tools: ruling pen (top) and glass cutter (bottom).

Cutting glass

Although it is better for the amateur to buy glass already cut to size, you may need to cut the occasional small piece of glass – perhaps when reducing the size of a frame or re-using the glass from an old frame – so it is worthwhile having the equipment for cutting your own glass.

There are many **glass cutters** to choose from, but I have found the best is the oil-filled type, because the cutting wheel is continually lubricated when in use. Although more expensive, this makes cutting smoother and gives a longer life than the standard six-wheel type.

A wooden or metal **T-square** is used to guide the glass cutter and the glass can be broken by hand or across an edge. For nibbling off thin slivers of glass, a pair of square-jawed glazier's pliers is absolutely invaluable.

Frame assembly

Even the slightest speck of dust can ruin a picture frame and you need a good glass cleaner. There are many proprietary brands of glass cleaner available and I have found that all of them work very well. If you prefer to make your own, a mixture of half methylated spirits and half water works very well, too. If possible, use a lint-free cloth to apply the cleaner.

One piece of specialised equipment which makes frame assembly a lot easier is a **glazier's gun**. This fires triangular darts or small metal wedges into the frame to hold the backing board in place – much quicker and neater than hammering in panel pins. Try and acquire a block of metal about 3kg (7lb) in weight to hold against the frame while using the glazing gun to prevent the frame distorting or coming apart.

You can buy frame mouldings with different depths of rebate, which should be enough for most purposes, but if the backing board of a picture (or the 'stretcher' of an oil painting) protrudes above the back of the moulding, a different method of fixing has to be used. I find the most reliable way is to drive panel pins at an angle through the edge of the backing (or stretcher) into the moulding, but be careful to use pins of the right length otherwise they could come through the side of the moulding and ruin the job.

Where you have constructed a box frame (for housing a three-dimensional object), this can often be secured into the frame by using something like decorator's sealant, piped around the box with a gun – see my *Dried flowers* Project on page 100 for an illustration of this method used in practice.

Decoration and finishing

Most of the specialist tools you need for frame and mount decoration are described in the appropriate sections (starting on pages 54 and 68), but a 450mm (18in) clear plastic **draughtsman's rule** with both metric and imperial markings is a must and a good **ruling pen** for drawing ink lines in mount decoration is a worthwhile investment. Forget about felt-tip pens and technical ink pens, they just don't work in framing.

If you are going in for ink lining and washlining, a **corner marking gauge** is another essential tool. This fits into the corner of a bevelled mount and allows you to mark exactly how far out from the window each line will be.

Decorating mounts and frames inevitably involves a fair selection of inks, paints, stains, paint brushes, cloths, sponges and the like. Fine wire wool is useful for applying waxes and a wire brush useful for opening up the grain.

As with other aspects of picture framing, you get what you pay for when buying materials – it is best to buy most decorating materials from a quality art shop.

You will need **wood filler** in various colours for filling in nail holes and any damage – **touch-up pens** for frame corners are useful and come in all stain finishes.

Extra equipment

Apart from the obvious tools that any practical workshop should have – such as a hammer, pliers, pincers and steel tape measure – a **staple gun** is essential for quick stretching of fabric and tapestries. For various fixing duties, such as sticking mounts together, a double-sided tape dispenser is also well worth having on the bench.

Taking it professionally

If you decide to get more serious about picture framing, you may well have to invest in some more expensive equipment.

First on the list comes a **guillotine cutter**. This 'chops' through the wood in a fraction of the time it takes to saw by hand, leaving perfectly finished mitres.

Next is a floor-standing **underpinner** – more robust than a bench-operated tool, it is also much quicker and easier to use as the clamp is built into the machine and the wedges are fed automatically.

Third comes a bench-mounted **mount cutter** with graduated scales, making the whole business of cutting mounts simpler and more accurate.

Finally, you might want to invest in a **rotary cutter** or bench-mounted guillotine for cutting mount-boards and backing boards.

Picture frame moulding

The main characteristic of the moulding used for picture framing is the rebate which holds the glass/mount/picture/backing board 'sandwich' in place. This can vary in both width and depth. Mouldings divide neatly into two groups – plain and decorated (finished). A plain moulding is made from wood and can be left in its natural state or finished as you wish – varnish, paint, stain or a paint or other effect (all of which we detail later in the book). A selection of plain mouldings is illustrated on pages 34 and 35.

A decorated moulding, on the other hand, is already finished for you and consequently will usually cost more. Most are made from wood, but some are based on metal or extruded plastic. See pages 36 and 37 for examples.

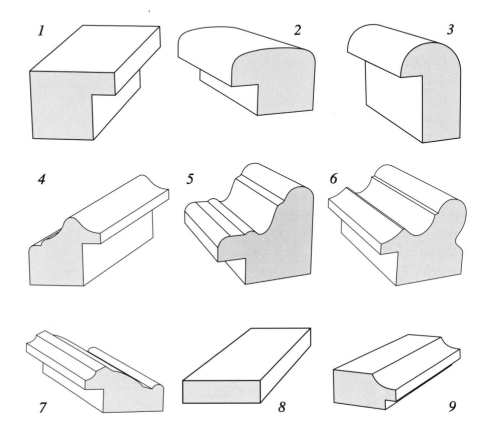

Moulding patterns

The drawings above show some of the main 'profiles' used for picture frame mouldings. These are by no means the only ones you will find – one supplier could have as many as 50 different profiles in different sizes and in different woods.

Flat (also known as **Square**) is basically what it says and is usually in small sections.

Cushion is a flat moulding with rounded corners or a rounded top.

Hockey-stick has a pronounced rounded top almost semi-circular in shape.

'Gothic' is one of the many moulding shapes available – typically with a convex central section.

Spoon is a profile with a curved concave centre 'spooned' out of it and is widely used in a variety of designs. **Scoop** is similar, but usually more ornate and sometimes undercut or with a 'fancy' back.

Reverse is the name given to a moulding where the outer edge is

Some of the moulding profiles available:
1. Flat
2. Cushion
3. Hockey-stick
4. 'Gothic'
5. Spoon
6. Scoop
7. Reverse
8. Flat slip
9. Bevel slip

thinner than the inner (rebate) edge. Its main value is a deep rebate, allowing the use of composite mounts. Available in several different profiles.
Flat slip is a non-rebated moulding, with a square or scalloped edge, for use with rebated moulding, usually to add an extra gold edge.
Slip and **bevel slip** are special rebated slips designed for use with other mouldings, sometimes with a material, such as linen or velvet.

Making your own moulding

With such a good choice of different timber profiles in the DIY stores, it is quite easy to make up your own mouldings, which you could then decorate in the way you want. These mouldings, of course, do not have the necessary rebate so, once you have selected the profile that you want for the top surface of the moulding, you need to find a length of square or rectangular planed timber, that is between 5 and 10mm (³⁄₁₆ to ³⁄₈in) less than the width of the chosen moulding – the other dimension will determine the depth of the rebate.

Decide which is to be the 'sight edge' of the moulding (i.e. which way round it is to be used) and apply wood adhesive to the underside and to the top of the square or rectangular timber, carefully aligning the outer edges. Secure the entire assembly with tape and leave for the adhesive to dry, before removing the tape and trimming the joint line with sandpaper and, if necessary, removing adhesive from the rebate with a trimming knife.

Some DIY stores and art shops will also sell ready-made frames in standard sizes for you to decorate in the way you want.

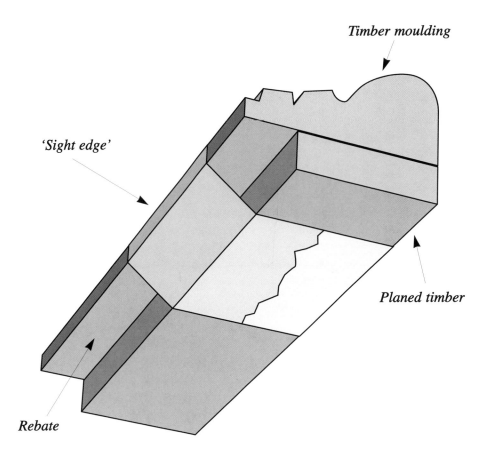

Timber moulding

'Sight edge'

Planed timber

Rebate

Making your own picture frame moulding using DIY moulding plus planed timber.

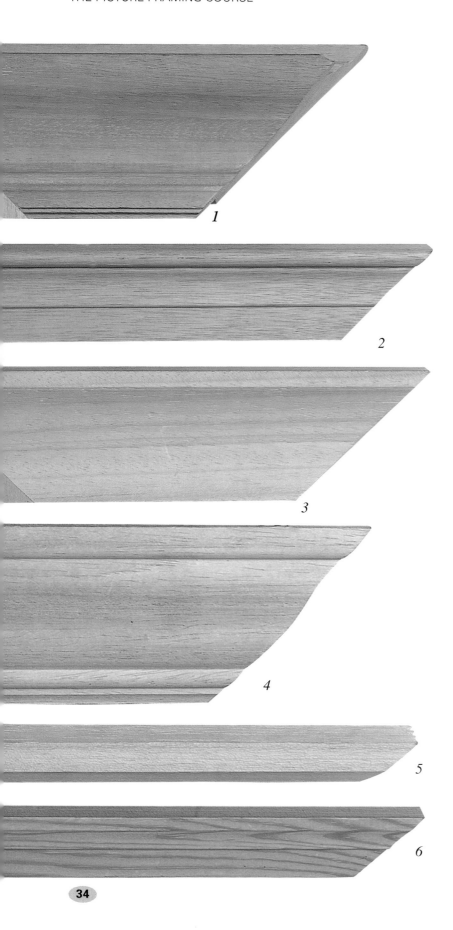

1

2

3

4

5

6

Plain mouldings

Although many different types of wood can be used for plain picture frame mouldings, three predominate – ramin, obeche and pine. All three are ideal in that they are free from defects, are stable and will not warp or twist.

Ramin is a creamy-white hardwood and has a fine, even texture with a close, shallow grain. It is excellent for cutting and is widely used for both ornate finishes and also embossed designs. Its main disadvantage is that it has a tendency to shrink

Obeche, another hardwood, is a straw colour. It is also good for cutting, but the grain is slightly more open than ramin. Obeche is less likely to shrink, and is therefore very widely used.

Pine is a softwood and is generally admired for its 'knotty' finish. It is used for more specific types of wood effect finishes than ramin and obeche and is therefore more limited in its application. It is the best of the three for taking stained natural wood finishes.

Some of the other woods used for picture framing include oak (with its distinctive grain) and maple, which has an attractive 'figure' on the surface. Oak is particularly appropriate for the technique of liming, where white wax is forced into the open grain.

A selection of plain mouldings

Left:

1. 3$\frac{1}{2}$in obeche scoop
2. 1$\frac{3}{4}$in ramin spoon
3. 2$\frac{1}{2}$in obeche shallow scoop
4. 3in obeche reverse
5. 1in obeche bevel slip
6. 1$\frac{1}{8}$in pine small slip

Right:

7. 3$\frac{5}{8}$in obeche reverse
8. 2in oak ridge flat
9. 1$\frac{3}{4}$in pine scoop
10. 1in maple veneer
11. $\frac{5}{8}$in ramin square
12. $\frac{5}{8}$in oak gothic
13. $\frac{3}{4}$in ramin hockey-stick

7

8

9

10

11

12

13

Decorated mouldings

Decorated picture frame mouldings, available from specialist suppliers, come in an enormous range of colours and finishes – for example, painted, gilded, limed, lacquered or with a coloured plastic 'composite' finish. There is no practical problem working with any of these, except that you may need some touch-up pens for repairing scratches and damaged corners. You can, however, also get mouldings with a definite pattern embossed into them – either pressed into the wood itself or added on to a base profile. Impressed mouldings are of a relatively simple and shallow design and are usually the easiest to work with.

Decoration added to a base profile will either be a plaster-type compound or a combination of veneers arranged in a pattern. The plaster compound is the one used for the more ornate and flowery patterns. Care should be taken when cutting this type of moulding, as problems can occur with flaking and chipping of the compound and some filling may be necessary, using a proprietary brand of general purpose cellulose filler. Veneered mouldings present no problems and should be treated in exactly the same way as plain mouldings.

A selection of decorated
mouldings:
Left:
1. Reverse wood and gold
2. Antique gold shallow scoop
3. Antique gold
4. Plastic-covered scoop gold
5. Reverse antique floral pine
6. Green hump wash
7. Bright red composition
8. Gold slip
9. Pink composition
10. Gold slip

Right:
11. Spoon and gold
12. Scoop gold and green lines
13. Gold stress reverse
14. Brown two gold lines
15. Plastic-covered floral reverse
16. Brown hump wash
17. Brown embossed reverse
18. Round blue and gold
19. Reverse green wash
20. Dark blue composition

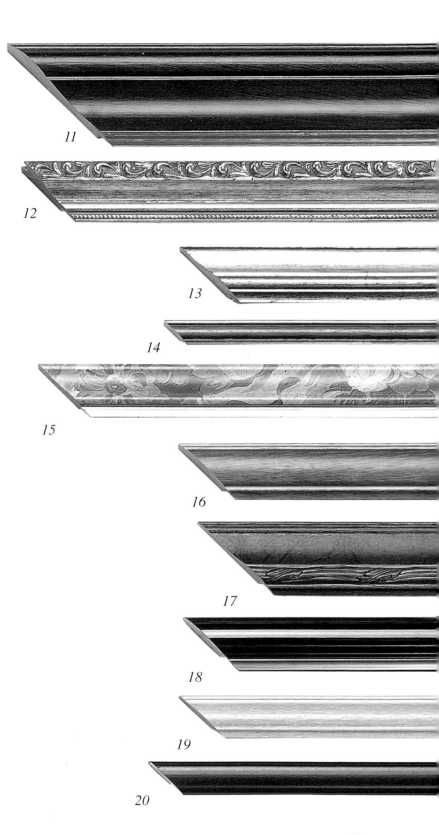

Mount-board, glass and backing

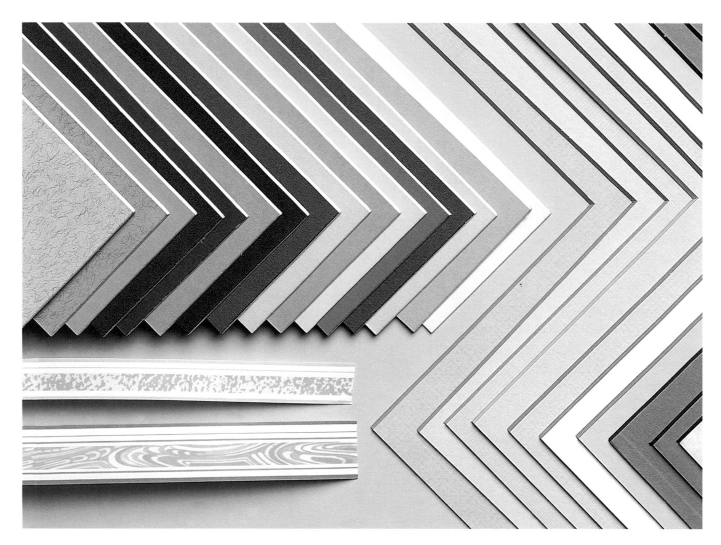

Mount-board

The range of mount-board available to the framer is awesome, both from picture framing suppliers and from art shops. By far the most common is a pale ivory board with a white core which is exposed when a bevel is cut in the mount. But you can get a whole range of colours and also board with a black or coloured core for a more dramatic lead-in to a picture – though, of course, you can paint a white exposed core any colour you want.

As well as boards with a 'paper' finish, you can get an embossed linen finish or ones which have already been covered in fabric. Browsing through the samples at a

A typical selection of the mount-boards available. In addition to the traditional mount-boards with white cores (top left), you can get boards with both black and coloured cores (right). At the bottom left are shown self-adhesive decorative strips.

supplier will give you an idea of the range of types available.

Most mount-board consists of several sheets of paper laminated together – normally six, to give '6-sheet' paper, which is about 2mm, or just over $\frac{1}{16}$ in, thick. This is more than thick enough when you are cutting a 45° bevel in it and some companies produce a thinner 4-sheet board which is perhaps worth considering, but it is advisable to balance ease of cutting with the stiffness of the board; the larger the mount, the more it is liable to buckle in the frame if cut from thinner board.

Mount-board is sold in standard sheet sizes of 44in by 32in (1117mm by 813mm). Most have an 'acid-free' backing sheet to protect the artwork; more expensive 'conservation' boards have been chemically treated to make them inert. For protecting really valuable pictures, many framers will use rag-pulp (cotton fibre) mount-board.

Glass

Picture framing glass is thinner (2mm) and more fragile than glass used in house windows and is usually sold in 'half sheets' 4ft by 3ft (1220mm by 914mm) as full-size sheets are far too difficult and dangerous to handle.

For most pictures you will want to use clear glass, but sometimes diffuse – or non-reflective – glass may be more appropriate. This has the advantage that any light falling on to the picture (from a window or light bulb) is not reflected, but the disadvantage that the picture itself is less clear. The further behind the glass the picture is, the more diffused is the light coming from it, so non-reflective glass should not normally be used where the picture has a mount and the general rule should be only to use it on 'close' framing (no mount).

The four main components of a finished picture frame. Mitred moulding (here joined by underpinning), a bevelled edge coloured mount-board, hardboard backing and glass (ready to be cleaned).

Backing board

Backing board comes in various guises and each framer has his own particular favourite. The most popular by far is 2mm hardboard, which is widely available. Unlike normal hardboard, which has one smooth and one rough side, picture framing hardboard is smooth both sides (SBS). However, it is not in my view a perfect material, being relatively heavy, difficult to cut, producing bits and dust and attracting moisture.

Among the alternatives (which include the latest MDF – medium-density fibreboard), my own particular favourite is grey pulp board. This comes in various thicknesses and therefore various degrees of stiffness, is easy to cut, dust and bit free and relatively dry. Another good choice is corrugated cardboard. Widely used in the USA, it is curiously little used in the UK. The absolute ideal backing board is foam-core. Very light, delightfully easy to cut, remarkably stiff and strong for its weight, it is absolutely stable and is as good as you can get for framing. Sadly it is relatively expensive.

Foam-core comes into its own when it comes to making box frames for housing a three-dimensional subject - see my *Dried Flowers* project on page 100 for more details of this.

Fixings

You will normally need fixings on the back of the frame so that you can hang a picture on the wall.

The most commonly used fixings for picture frames are screw eyes which are available in many different sizes, and simply screw into the frame with the aid of a pilot hole formed by a bradawl. I find that these tend to look rather clumsy, especially in the larger sizes, so I generally prefer to use chrome-plated or brass D-rings, which are fixed in place with a screw and lie flat against the back surface of the moulding. The most effective type of screw is the 'cheese-head' self-tapping type, between 9mm ($\frac{3}{8}$in) and 25mm (1in) in length. Larger D-rings are available with two fixing holes for heavy jobs.

Whether you use screw eyes or D-rings, suitable cord for hanging must be tied between them. There is a misinformed theory that picture wire is stronger than nylon cord. Initially, this is true; but most picture wire is brass-coated steel and, over a period of time, the core of the wire can rust and result in failure, giving fairly catastrophic and potentially dangerous results. If stronger material is required, use chain link which is much more reliable.

Some pictures need to be fixed permanently to the wall; for this it is necessary to use 'mirror' plates. These are brass plated with three holes in them; two holes for screwing the plate to the frame, and one for screwing into the wall. Mirror plates will not work if the backing board sticks out beyond the moulding, so if they are to be used, pay particular attention to the rebate depth of the moulding being used.

Mirror plates apart, there is a wide choice of picture hooks, picture pins and other hanging systems available – including the traditional hook over a picture rail. All of these are described in detail in the *Hanging Pictures* section, starting on page 116.

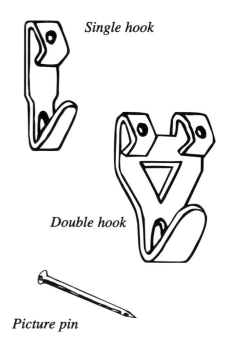

Single hook

Double hook

Picture pin

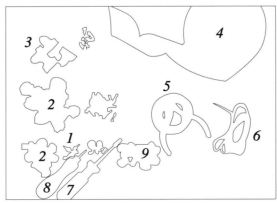

*Some of the tools and materials
used for finishing off pictures:*
1. *Screw eyes*
2. *Chrome-plated D-rings*
3. *Mirror plates and screws*
4. *Sticky brown paper*
5. *Picture wire and wire cutters*
6. *Nylon cord*
7. *Screwdriver*
8. *Bradawl*
9. *Brass D-rings*

Basic techniques

There are two distinct skills needed in picture framing. The first is the ability to carry out detailed craft work – cutting mitres in wood, cutting accurate bevels in mount-board and so on – and the second is an artistic ability – not just the decoration of frames and mounts but a good 'eye' for colour and proportions. Many people find that one or other of these skills comes more easily to them, but all the basic techniques needed for picture framing can be learnt and – with patience and practice – perfected.

A place to work

For framing pictures – and for decorating mounts, mouldings and frames – the ideal is to have a dedicated space, perhaps a spare bedroom or unused dining room.

But not everyone has the space they can give up to this and will have to make do using existing space in a different way.

You actually need two different spaces – one for the 'dirty' jobs (especially cutting and joining mouldings and, if you attempt it, cutting glass) and one for the 'clean' jobs (especially mount decoration and final assembly). You need a warm well-lit area for both, but a possible compromise is to do the 'dirty' work in the garage or garden shed and the 'clean' work on the kitchen table or dining room table, storing the tools and equipment as appropriate – but make sure that timber mouldings are stored in a dry space.

In both areas of work, some kind of vacuum cleaner is essential – even a small hand-held one – to hoover up sawdust and slivers of mount-board and decorative paper; most picture framers make their working area a non-smoking, non-eating and non-drinking area.

Wherever you work, try to make maximum use of natural daylight and ensure you are never working in your own shadow.

The dedicated workshop

If you do have the space to turn a spare bedroom into your picture framing 'workshop', keep the same principle in mind – one half of the room for 'dirty' work and one half (preferably the half nearest the window) for 'clean' work. Getting the right layout is important not just for cleanliness but also for ensuring a smooth flow of work. To begin with, the main assembly bench should ideally be an 'island' which you can walk round completely. When deciding on the size of the bench, bear in mind that the typical construction material – i.e. chipboard, plywood or MDF (medium-density fibreboard) – comes in 8ft x 4ft sheets, which is more or less the ideal size.

For optimum working efficiency, mount a corner clamp (mitre vice) in one corner, so that the upper surface of the vice support area is level with the bench, thus giving the maximum support possible to the frame, and mount a hand-operated mitre saw into an adjoining corner with a hand-operated underpinner in a third corner, preferably let into the bench so that the picture frame will be supported on the bench surface. When positioning the saw, remember that you may need to support long lengths of moulding to one side or the other.

A second 'decorative' working area could then be created against the wall under the window, as far away from the mitre saw as possible and with a good electric light for working after dark.

Inevitably, a bench top tends to become cluttered with tools which get in the way. I have found that a good way of keeping the bench clear is to fix a length of plastic rainwater guttering to the edge of the bench, just below the work surface, and adjacent to where the main work is done. It is surprising how much this will swallow up, thus leaving the bench top clear.

Storage of moulding is not normally a problem for the amateur, as you can buy mouldings as and when you need them. But you will need a space for storing partially used lengths or lengths waiting to be cut – remember that most moulding is sold in lengths at least 2.7m (9ft) long.

Mount-board is best stored flat and a good place for this is under the workbench. Make sure the walls of the 'workshop' are well fitted with plenty of shelving as it is amazing how many pots of paints, inks, polishes, adhesives etc you can acquire over the years.

If you cut your own glass, this will mean having a safe place to store it – you do not want broken glass around the place.

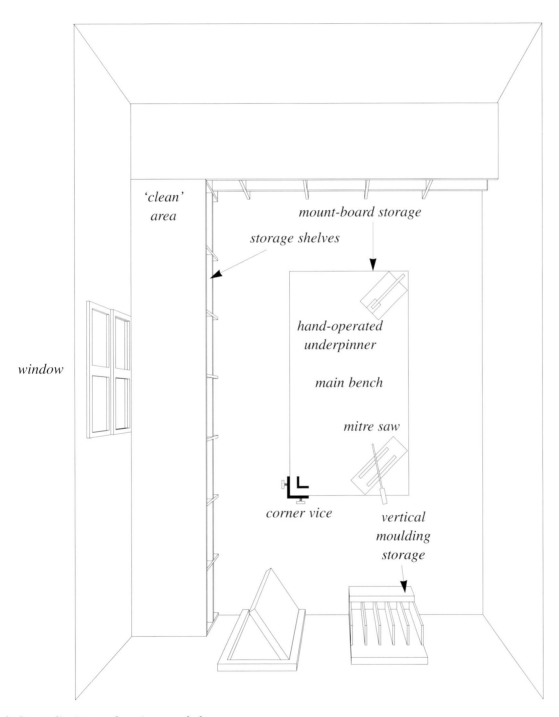

'clean' area

mount-board storage

storage shelves

hand-operated underpinner

main bench

mitre saw

window

corner vice

vertical moulding storage

A 'dedicated' picture framing workshop.

Mitre cutting

Cutting the moulding to make the frame is done after the mount has been cut to size. Only when you are happy with the size and proportions of this relative to the picture, should you start cutting the precious wood. To work out the lengths to cut the mouldings measure the length and width of the mount (or the picture and backing if no mount is being used), adding around 2mm (¹⁄₁₆in) for clearance and subtracting twice the width of the rebate to give the inside dimensions of the moulding.

The procedure is to cut the first piece of moulding and then to check it against the subject assembly and make any adjustments necessary and, if all is well, to cut the second matching piece to the same size. Always cut the longer sides first, because if you make a mistake you can always use the piece of moulding for one of the shorter sides. When the long sides have been cut, repeat the procedure for the shorter sides.

Using a mitre saw

The hand mitre saw is really a sophisticated mitre box, but all the positioning and running action of the saw is mechanically controlled and therefore much more precise.

Where possible, try to mount the saw assembly into the bench so that the bench top is level with the metal bed of the saw, so that the moulding is well supported and keep the moving parts and saw guide well lubricated to ensure constant ease of use.

This type of saw will have a ready-made location slot in the bed of the machine, allowing easy location of the cutting marks on the moulding, and better designs have a clamp for holding the moulding and perhaps a stop for positioning it for repeat cutting.

The order of cutting, with the moulding on your left and the rebate facing towards you, is first to cut a mitre from the left-hand side, then to re-position the moulding and cut the second mitre from the right-hand side – mark the correct cutting length on the moulding after cutting the first mitre before cutting the second.

When making the actual cut, concentrate on a steady and even stroke with the saw, remembering to use as much of the length of the saw blade as possible. Remember that with a hand-saw, the forward stroke is the cutting stroke, the rearward stroke is merely re-positioning for the next cutting stroke. To make the cutting easier, try rubbing a candle along the sides of the saw blade; the wax will give a helpful lubrication to the cutting, but won't stain the timber.

Using a mitre saw – step-by-step

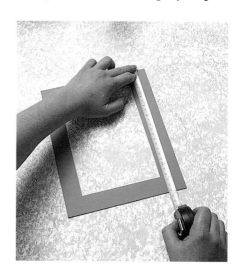

1 Measure the length of the mount-board, allowing 2mm (¹⁄₁₆in) for clearance and calculate the inside dimension of the frame.

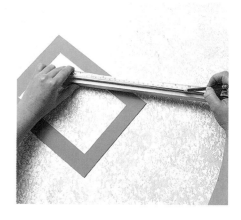

2 After cutting the first mitre, transfer the frame measurement to the moulding.

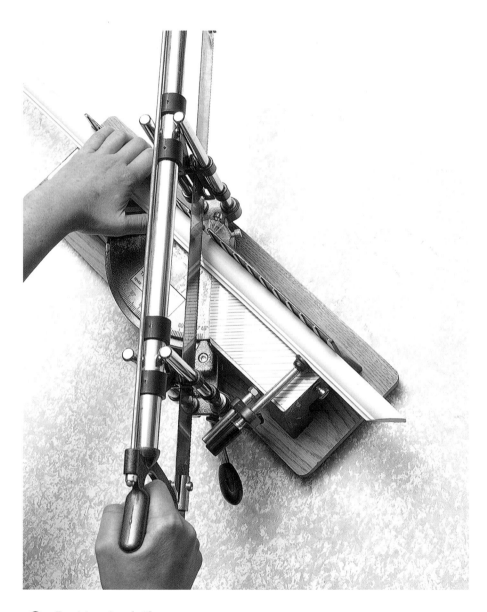

3 Position (and, if you can, clamp) the moulding in the saw and cut the second mitre.

4 Check the length of the moulding against the mount.

5 Remove any rough burrs gently with a razor blade or artist's scalpel.

Using a mitre box

Before starting the cut, it is a good practice to place a piece of flat, scrap, timber in the bottom of the box, and, preferably, fix it in place with a couple of screws. Then use a fine-toothed tenon saw to make saw cuts in this at both the 45° angles, thus giving an indication as to where the moulding can be positioned before cutting the actual mitres. The scrap base piece can be replaced when it is worn.

It is also a good idea to screw or clamp the mitre box to the bench, so that it does not move around while you are sawing – ideally, the bench surface should be level with the top of the wood insert which will allow the moulding to sit naturally level in the mitre box and require less effort to hold in place. The order of cutting is the same as for using a mitre saw – the golden rule is to 'let the saw do the work' – but because of the slight inherent inaccuracy of the mitre box, some filling of mitres may be necessary after assembly.

An L-shaped mitre block is used in the same way as a mitre box – again, you need a piece of scrap wood on which to rest the moulding as the saw cuts do not reach all the way down to the base. The photograph on page 28 shows a corner clamp which can be used for cutting mitres.

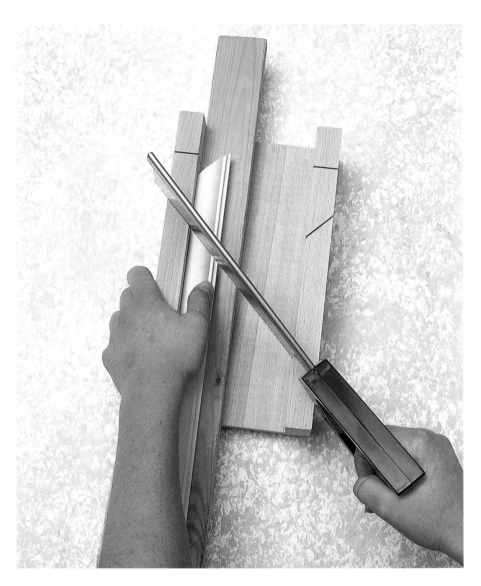

Making the first cut using a tenon saw and mitre box, with the moulding supported on a scrap of timber.

Frame joining

Once the mitres have been cut accurately, you are ready to assemble the frame. This is the point in the whole operation where one of the silliest mistakes is commonly made – that is, to get the longer and shorter lengths mixed up, with the result that you join two long lengths (or two short lengths) together and find you have two unequal halves of a frame that don't match!

It is a good idea to adopt a working method that prevents this and stick to it: my own personal formula is Long Left – in other words, when assembling the frame, I always work with the longest pieces of moulding on my left-hand side.

Joining with adhesive and pins

Very accurate mitres are required for this, but it is quite easy, on smaller frames, to apply the PVA woodworking adhesive to the mitres and then, on a flat surface, to assemble the four pieces together and pass a strong rubber band around the perimeter of the frame and weight the corners. Leave for a few hours, and a reasonable job should result.

For larger frames you will need some kind of clamp and, when using a clamp, it is essential to

work on a clear, flat surface. Before applying the clamp to the four pieces of moulding, apply the PVA wood adhesive to one side of the two mitres at each corner. On some softer mouldings, where the wood has a rather open grain, it is

The picture framing clamp is tightened by a ratchet knob. Additional corner pieces are available for hexagonal and octagonal frames.

sometimes advisable to glaze the mitres first by applying a preliminary coat of PVA adhesive to each of the mitres and allowing it to dry before applying the final joining coat. This seals the end grain of the timber, preventing excessive soaking away of the adhesive. Have some heavy objects ready to weight down the corners, so that potential warping or twisting is avoided.

Immediately after applying the adhesive to the mitres, assemble the four pieces of moulding together and apply the clamp. When the clamp is tightened and the moulding correctly positioned, wipe away any excess adhesive with a damp cloth. Weight the corners down and leave for the adhesive to set.

The corners should then be reinforced with pins as described below in *Using a corner clamp* and the nail holes and any gaps in the mitres filled.

Support the frame well when hammering in the pins – these provide more support if put in the sides, but are less visible if put in the top and bottom.

Using a corner clamp

If you are using a corner clamp (mitre vice), assemble the frame in two halves (one short and one long piece) and then join the two halves together. Position the two pieces in the clamp until the mitre matches perfectly. Then remove one piece and apply PVA wood adhesive to the mitre surface, replace in the vice and tighten firmly.

Use holding pins or veneer pins to secure the corners, not panel pins as these are too thick. Do not attempt to hammer the pins directly into the moulding as this is usually hard work, may bend the pin and can result in the wood splitting. Instead, drill a pilot hole right through the outer moulding, so that the pin enters easily, and partway into the inner moulding. Use one of the pins to make the hole – simply snip the head off the pin and fasten it in the chuck of a hand-operated or electric drill. This is much cheaper than using fine drills and, of course, the hole is exactly the right size.

Before putting each pin in, dip its point into a small pot of thin oil near the vice – this will help it go in easily. Also have a narrow nail-driving punch handy to drive the head of the pin below the surface of the moulding. Before removing the corner from the vice, fill the holes with matching wood filler and rub away any excess. Any trimming, sanding and filling of the mitre corner can be done at this stage too.

Frame joining with a corner clamp – step-by-step

1 To avoid confusion when joining, keep the long pieces to the left, short to the right.

4 A cut-off pin is used for drilling a pilot hole ...

2 Apply adhesive to one side of the corner.

3 Tighten up the corner vice to hold the first two pieces of moulding square.

5 ... after which, the pins can be hammered into place.

6 A narrow nail punch is used to drive the nail heads in.

7 Filling the nail holes with matching wood filler.

Using an underpinner

Whilst it is usually a distinct advantage to use an underpinner, not all mouldings are suitable. As the moulding has to be clamped in place while the wedges are driven in, you should avoid using an underpinner on uneven mouldings such as reverse types or deep spoon profiles which could tilt in the clamp. Also to be avoided are hard woods such as oak and ash as the machine will simply not be up to the task.

When using an underpinner, adopt the same operating procedure as for the other methods of joining.

The underpinner drives metal wedges into the back of the frame – for mouldings up to 12mm (½in) wide, use one wedge; from 12mm to 20mm (¾in) use two and above that three, this being the real maximum needed on any width of moulding. The size of the wedges used depends of course on the thickness of the moulding. I believe the maximum depth or wedge available is 15mm (⅝in), but the largest generally used is more likely to be 10mm (⅜in). On very deep mouldings, a second wedge can be driven in behind the first one, so that they are 'stacked' one on top of the other.

Avoid driving wedges nearer than 3mm (⅛in) from the edges of the moulding as this can result in

Using an underpinner – step-by-step

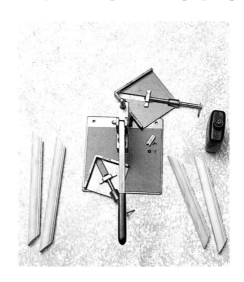

1 As with using a corner vice, keep long lengths to the left and short ones to the right.

2 Apply adhesive to one half of the joint.

splitting of the moulding near to the mitres and consequently an unsightly 'swelling' at the corners.

If you are uncertain whether the underpinner will work on a particular moulding, check first on two scrap mitred pieces. Make sure the wedges are driven just level with the underside of the moulding and ensure that the clamp is not marking the surface of the moulding. This can be either due to too much pressure by the operator or lack of cushioning on the clamp. If cushioning has to be added, try using cork as this is pliant yet firm.

5 Once two L-shapes have been made, the whole frame can be joined.

3 *With a hand-held underpinner, the two pieces of moulding are held in a special corner vice.*

6 *Use a moistened cloth to remove any excess adhesive at the corners.*

4 *With the moulding (and vice) upside down, wedges are driven in to secure the first corner.*

Frame decoration

Although you can buy a good selection of pre-decorated 'finished' mouldings, decorating your own mouldings using a little imagination and skill allows you to achieve a unique effect.

Most frame decoration is done on new or unfinished timber moulding, but this is not absolutely necessary: many good re-finishing jobs can be done on mouldings apparently already finished. In fact, this is one of my happiest jobs in the workshop – converting some nightmarish finish into a tasteful and expensive-looking frame.

When working on bare unfinished mouldings, it is essential that the wood surface is lightly rubbed down before you start and that any defects in the surface are repaired – cracks filled, for example.

Painting

Some of the best results in frame finishing are achieved with the use of paints. I have found water-based acrylic paints to be by far the best for the job and you can achieve a number of interesting effects by combining two colours – one as a base coat and the second as a wash over the top, which can then be rubbed so that the base coat shows through. After drying, polish with wax to give a good finish.

Experimentation is the key to some of the best and original ideas, but here are a few suggestions. 'Red clay' base with a diluted wash of black, then rubbed so that the red shows through the black, will give a nice 'mahogany'-type finish as shown here. Similarly, a 'chocolate' base washed with black and rubbed gives a dark oak effect whilst a sand gold base with a rubbed chocolate wash gives the appearance of antique pine.

Mahogany finish – step-by-step

The object here is to produce a frame that looks like a Victorian carved mahogany antique, which goes particularly well with old photographs. The best moulding to use is a simple large hockey-stick profile, which has been covered with a moulded paste finish already.

1 *Cut and join the mouldings, paying particular attention to blending the moulded paste at the corners with sandpaper.*

2 *Give the frame two coats of red acrylic paint allowing it to dry between coats.*

3 *Now prepare a solution of
50% black or antique brown
acrylic paint and 50% water and
wash this over the frame using a
brush, allowing the colour to settle
in the hollows of the 'carved'
decoration.*

4 *When completely dry, take a
damp cloth and rub the top
surfaces of the decoration until
the red shows through, giving the
mahogany effect. Finally, apply
silicone furniture polish to the
entire frame using a soft brush
and allow to dry. When buffed
to a shine and finished the
effect is quite authentic and
very impressive.*

Liming

This is a technique which enhances the grain of wood and is therefore best used on open-grained woods such as oak. The effect can be enhanced by opening the grain up even further using a wire brush. Most of the work is done on the mitred mouldings before they are assembled into a frame.

For liming, you will need some liming wax which is readily available. You will find the procedure quite simple.

First of all, the wood is stained to the colour you want using a water-based stain and then the surface sealed with a pale or white 'brushing' French polish (to ensure the liming wax is not patchy) and allowed to dry.

The liming wax is applied with wire wool, working across the grain of the wood: wipe off any surplus with a soft cloth dipped in white spirit.

After assembling the frame, use a dry cloth first across and then along the grain to leave just the pores filled. Allow to dry overnight before finishing with a wax polish.

Liming – step-by-step

1 For maximum effect, open up the grain of the mouldings using a wire brush.

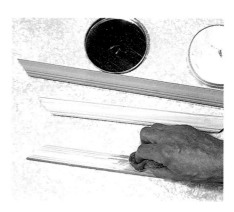

2 Stain the moulding if required and apply liming wax with wire wool, working it well into the grain.

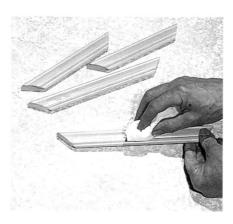

3 Wipe off surplus liming wax with a soft cloth soaked in white spirit.

4 Assemble the frame and finish off with a dry cloth. When dry apply a wax polish.

Staining

For staining plain wood, you can get two sorts of stain (dye) – water-based stains, available in a range of colours (including bright yellows, reds and blues), and spirit-based stains, available mainly in timber colours. Spirit-based stains can be quicker to use, as the water-based ones tend to 'raise the grain' on some softer timbers which means you have to spend time rubbing the surface down.

A water-based stain comes as a powder which you mix with water – so you can vary the intensity of the colour by varying the amount of water used and create your own colours by mixing stains together. It is best applied with a soft cloth as it is quite difficult to get even coverage with a brush. Use a fine grade of garnet paper to rub down the surface if the grain has been raised.

A soft cloth is also used to apply a spirit-based stain, working quickly so that the colour is even. The stain comes ready-mixed, but can be diluted with white spirit for a paler effect or you could mix two colours together. Try to use stain colours in keeping with the timber being used: do not use an oak stain on a pine moulding, for instance; similarly a pine stain probably would not have much effect on oak moulding.

Always stain before mitring, as staining afterwards can result in darkened mitres which look unsightly. When the stain has dried, seal the surface with varnish or brushing French polish.

Waxing

There are two main types of wax you can use to finish a picture frame – French polish (shellac) and wax polish (a mixture of carnauba wax and beeswax). French polish is normally applied with a 'rubber' (a cloth wrapped around a cotton wool pad), but is also sold in a grade suitable for applying with a brush and only twenty minutes need be left between coats. It provides a good seal to the timber.

Wax polish itself can be applied with a brush or with very fine grade (0000) wire wool and then polished with a soft cloth to give a lustrous finish.

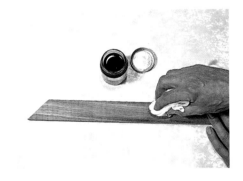

Applying French polish with a cloth.

Applying a spirit-based dye.

Stippling and sponging

Stippling and sponging are both way of producing a 'mottled' colour effect on the finished frame – the difference is that stippling is done with a soft brush to dab on the paint and sponging is done using a natural sponge to apply the paint.

Some really stunning effects can be achieved by using paint in this way over a base colour and, again, your own imagination is the only limiting factor. Try mottling black over dark green to give a luscious 'jungle' effect, for example, or dark brown over terracotta to give a 'bird's-eye maple' look. A moulding with raised lines or 'reveals' on it can be used to achieve some interesting shaded effects - for example, a base coat of sand gold covered with dilute pale grey applied with a brush along the edge of the reveal will give a 'dusty' look once the excess has been wiped away with a damp cloth. Or try the same base (sand gold) with dark brown instead of grey for an 'antiqued' effect.

To sponge paint, you will need a natural sponge and some acrylic paint – though you could also use oil-based paints or water-based emulsion paints. If you are working on a bare moulding, start by applying a base coat with a brush and allow to dry. Then prepare the coloured paint of your choice, diluting it if required, and take a natural sponge with a good 'spiky' texture and dip it in the paint. 'Bounce' the sponge all over the surface randomly to give a mottled appearance. If you want, repeat with a different colour. Some experimentation with different sponges and different paints will bring rich and imaginative rewards.

The sponging technique can be used over the whole frame (before it is assembled), but is particularly effective when used on a plain 'slip' which fits around the inside of the frame. The slip is assembled by mitring the corners in the same way as for making a basic frame.

To stipple, you prepare the surface and apply the first base coat in the same way, but this time use a soft-haired brush, similar to a shoe-shining brush, either to apply the second paint colour or to break it up after you have applied it with a normal brush.

Sponging – step-by-step

1 After mitring the moulding, paint it with a base colour using a brush.

3 *Repeat the procedure with a diluted green acrylic paint on top of the red.*

2 *Allow the base coat to dry and prepare a dilution of red acrylic paint, about 1 part paint to 3 parts water and apply to the moulding with a sponge.*

4 *The result is a very attractive 'garland of roses' effect.*

Spattering

This is another technique using two or more different paint colours. The first base coat is applied with a fine brush and the final coat is then 'flicked' on to the surface, either by running your thumb along an old nail-brush or tooth-brush dipped in paint or by tapping a brush loaded with paint against a wooden stick (or the handle of another brush). For example, to produce an 'olde' gold look, seal a moulding with a base coat of solid red acrylic, paint with gilt paint, allow to dry, sponge with diluted dark brown and spatter with diluted black paint.

Spattering – step-by-step

1 Sealing the moulding with red acrylic paint.

2 Applying a gilt paint on top (rub if required when dry to allow some of the red to show).

3 'Sponging' on diluted antique brown paint.

4 Spattering on diluted black paint by flicking it from an old nail-brush.

Decorating a frame with paper

The 'sponging' technique can be adapted to make your own decorated paper to cover frame moulding. Use plain mouldings for covering, such as cushion and hockey-stick profiles. Almost any type of paper can be used for this as long as it is not too thick.

Prepare the paper in sheets as long as is practicable and tape it down on a board, so that the surface will not wrinkle when using the sponging technique to achieve the mottled effect.

When you have achieved the mottled effect you want, cut the paper from the board in strips, after carefully measuring around the profile of the moulding to establish the width needed. Allow an extra 12mm (½in) for wrapping round the rebate and base. Apply PVA adhesive to the rebate edge of the moulding first and stick one edge of the strip of the paper firmly on this. When this is firmly stuck, apply adhesive to the rest of the profile and wrap the paper tightly around it. Finally, apply adhesive to the base of the moulding and wrap the remainder of the paper around on to this. Now mitre and assemble the moulding in the same way as for a basic frame.

The same technique could be used with pre-decorated paper – marbled paper, for example – cut into appropriately sized strips. This technique, illustrated here, is particularly effective on mouldings which have a flat (or gently curved) central section. Using this method, you should mitre the moulding first of all.

Decorating with paper – step-by-step

1 Cut the paper into strips to fit the moulding.

2 Apply PVA adhesive to the back of the paper.

3 Stick the paper down on to the moulding and trim ends.

4 A custom-made decorated frame.

Mount cutting

One of the most important decisions in picture framing is whether or not to use a mount and, if so, what its size should be relative to the size of the picture or photograph being framed.

Most pictures benefit from a mount, which draws the eye into the picture and which also ' spaces' the picture visually from, for example, highly patterned wallpaper. A light-coloured mount can make a dark picture seem smaller, whilst a dark mount around a light-coloured picture can make it look bigger. And, of course, the mount keeps the picture away from the glass.

The size of mount you choose depends very much on the actual piece being framed. Sometimes, the mount needs to be no more than a narrow border around the picture, whilst with a very small picture a really dramatic effect can be achieved by using a much larger frame with the mount making up the difference.

It really is a matter of personal preference and you should always experiment with offcuts of mounts in different colours (to contrast with or to echo the colours in the picture itself) in different sizes until you are happy with the overall proportions in combination with the frame moulding you are using. It is, however, worth pointing out

at this stage that when cutting a mount, you should always make the bottom border wider than the top and sides in order to create the correct visual balance – if it is the same size, it actually looks smaller. This difference does not need to be much – around 6 to 10mm (¼ to ⅜in) is usually sufficient.

Cutting the mount to size

The first operation is to cut the mount to its finished size: the cutting lines for this can be marked on the front of the mount board (the pencil line will be covered by the frame afterwards). Cutting to size is simple to do with a trimming knife held against a straight-edge with the mount-board supported on a self-healing mat or a mount-board offcut. For safety's sake, keep the cutting line away from your body and, when cutting, keep the straight-edge firmly pressed down and the knife firmly against it.

When you have decided the size of the aperture required in the mount, and the width of the borders (remembering the visual 'balance' at the bottom), mark these sizes out on the back of the prepared mount-board, using a fine pencil and a draughtsman's plastic ruler. A set square, T-square (or carpenter's try square) will ensure 90° corners.

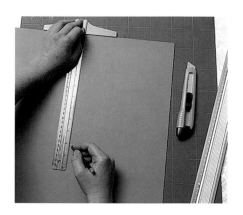

1 *A T-square will ensure 90° corners when marking out.*

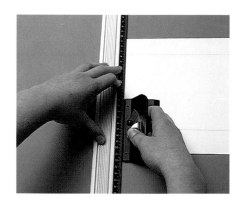

4 *Start the cut by lining up the mark on the mount cutter and pressing the blade down into the board.*

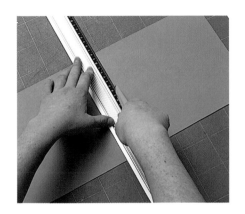

2 *Use a trimming knife for cutting the mount to size.*

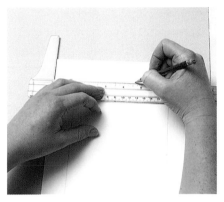

3 *The 'window' is marked on the back of the board.*

5 *Push the cutter firmly along the straight-edge until the mark meets the far line.*

6 *If necessary, clean up the corners using a razor blade or artist's scalpel.*

Cutting the aperture

Although you can do it either way round, it is best to cut a bevelled aperture from the back of the mount-board – in this way your start and finish pencil lines do not have to be removed afterwards. But you need to take care to check that you are always cutting the bevel the correct way round – that is, leading into the picture (and, incidentally, preventing any shadows which you can get with a square cut mount).

The first thing to do is to set the depth of the blade of your hand-held mount cutter so that it just cuts through the mount-board being used. Then position the straight-edge along the cutting line or just away from it so that the blade is on the line (with cutters like this, it helps to have a small piece of board cut to exactly this distance so that you can always use it to position the straight-edge). As it is difficult to hold the straight-edge and use the mount cutter at the same time, it helps if you can clamp the straight-edge down on to the bench.

The bevel is cut in one firm stroke after first lowering the cutting blade down through the mount-board at the first corner, but you need to take great care when you reach the next corner. Because you are cutting a bevel of 45° from

the back of the board, you need to start and finish slightly in front of the corner marks to compensate for the thickness of the board. In the case of '6-sheet' mount-board, this distance is about 3mm (⅛in), but if you overcut you will leave a visible line on the front of the mount-board. Practice makes perfect and you should always have a trial run on a piece of scrap mount-board first. Better quality mount cutters have a line marked on them showing you where to start and stop the cut.

When you have cut all four sides of the aperture, the 'window' should drop out, but if the cuts are not quite complete at the corners (and this is more desirable than overcuts), finish the cut with a very thin, double-sided razor blade or artist's scalpel. As a finishing touch, rub down the slight edge on the top of the bevel cut with a hard smooth edge. If you have made a slight error, use a fine emery board (the type sold for shaping finger nails) to smooth away the damage.

Cutting circles and ovals

Sometimes, a circular or oval 'window' may be more appropriate – especially when framing photographs of people – and one advantage of using a hand-held mount cutter is that it can be used

for cutting curves. To do this, you will first of all need to make yourself a plywood or card template around which the hand-held mount cutter can be guided.

A circle can be marked out with a pair of compasses or with a pencil on the end of a piece of thread working round a pin in the centre of the circle. An oval can also be marked out with pins, pencil and string, but is a little more involved. If you know the size of oval you want (i.e. the maximum length and width), start by drawing these two lines on the card as a cross, making sure the centre of the cross is where you want it. Measure the longest distance (L) and draw lines from the end of the shortest line of half this distance (½ L) so that they meet the longest line, forming a triangle. To minimise error, repeat from the other end of the shortest line. Now insert two pins at these points and cut and knot a loop of thread such that when it is wound around one pin, a pencil put in the loop will be exactly at the other end of the longest line. The pencil can then be used to draw the oval, running it round inside the loop and keeping the thread taut the whole time.

When you are happy with the shape of the template (the edge may take a bit of smoothing to get right), position it correctly on the mount-board and cut very carefully around it, ensuring the mount cutter stays in correct contact with the template – something which is easier to do if you can see the blade of the mount cutter.

It has to be said, however, that cutting oval or round apertures like this takes a lot of skill and practice and, to begin with, you would be better off buying special mounts which already have the circle or oval cut in them.

If you think you might be cutting a lot of ovals or circles in the future, it could be worth investing in a special hand-held oval mount cutter. Although fairly expensive, this tool does make the task very much simpler.

Using an oval mount cutter – step-by-step

1 Mark out the centre of the circle or oval on the front of the mount board and set the width and length of the oval on mount cutter.

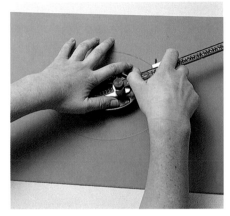

2 Position the mount cutter at the centre of the oval and make the cut progressively lowering the blade one notch at a time.

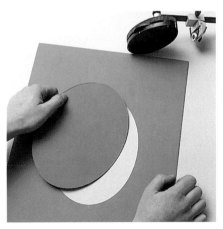

3 Lift out the 'window' and make good any damage.

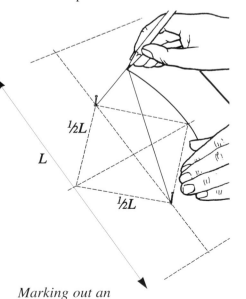

½L

L

½L

Marking out an oval using pins and string.

Cutting a double mount

A double mount gives you the opportunity to use two different colours of mount-board, one on top of the other with two different sizes of aperture. This is particularly valuable when you want to use a strong mount-board colour which could overpower the picture on its own but, with a double mount, the strong colour can be used to give a thin band around the inner edge of the 'window'.

Start by cutting the outer mount, using the same measuring method as for a single mount and cutting the window larger (by whatever amount you decide) than the window for the inner mount. Do not remove the window, but apply a piece of double-sided adhesive tape to the back of it with more double-sided adhesive tape around the window (all on the back of the board). Cut the second piece of board, of the required contrasting colour, slightly smaller – about 6mm (¼in) all round – and stick this to the back of the first piece, positioning it centrally. Now mark out the inner window, measuring from the outer edges of the first piece and cut out the second window. Both windows can now be removed together.

You could extend this technique to triple mounts – but try to make sure the steps between the mounts are not all the same.

Cutting a double mount – step-by-step

1 Cut the window in the outer mount (usually the lighter colour) and apply double-sided adhesive tape to the back of this mount.

2 Replace the window of the outer mount (holding it in place with more double-sided adhesive tape) and then stick the slightly smaller inner mount to the back of the outer mount.

3 Cut the window in the inner mount and remove both windows together.

'V'-groove mount

A 'V'-groove mount is exactly what it says, a mount with an additional 'V'-groove cut out in its surface, to provide a decorative effect by exposing the core of the mount-board.

First take a piece of mount-board of the size required and cut out the normal window. Decide where you want the 'V'-groove to be and mark this out on the back of the board. Cut to this line as if you were cutting a normal window, but do not remove the cut-out; instead tape it in place. Now turn the mount over so that it is face up. Taking great care, cut along inside the exposed line, creating a second bevel facing the other way, but make sure you do not cut too much off.

The same technique can be used with a double mount with the reverse bevel being cut further inside the first cut, allowing the underlying mount-board to show through as a band of colour framed on both sides by the core of the upper mount-board.

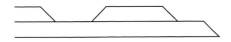

Cross-section of double mount with a wide V-groove.

1 Start by cutting the window in the mount as usual, and then make a second cut in the mount where you want the V-groove to be and tape the cut line before turning the board over.

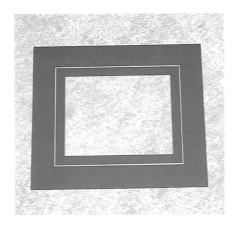

2 Working from the front of the board, cut carefully along inside the exposed line to create the V-groove.

Developing mounts further

So much more can be done with mounts over and above standard singles and doubles. Multi-mounts, for instance, can give very interesting effects, particularly when cut using solid colour rag-fibre board. Try starting with an oval, and then several rectangles, perhaps up to six, each one about 3mm (⅛in) larger than the last.

Combinations of ovals and rectangles are also visually exciting and again give a unique attraction to your particular style of framing. Try superimposing a rectangle on an oval, perhaps around an ordinary rectangle, again using solid rag in the same colour.

Mount decoration

Mount decoration is a subject particularly dear to my heart as I believe it is the real centre of interest of any framing job and also provides the greatest scope for innovation and design.

The most common method of decoration is the use of ink lines and 'washlines' (bands of delicate colour) that form a panel all the way around the border of the mount. This method is traditionally used for watercolours and prints, though carefully chosen ink lines and washlines can enhance many other types of picture.

Other techniques include the use of pre-decorated paper or fabric to cover all or part of the mount and various paint techniques – sponging, stippling, spattering, stencilling and so on.

Ink lines

A lot of mount decoration starts with ink lines. For these you will need a good quality ruling pen, a corner marking device and a straight-edge or ruler. The corner marking device allows you to mark out the spacing of lines from each corner. When buying one, choose the type which can be used with a pencil; the ones that punch holes in mounts are more trouble than they are worth.

Using a ruling pen is relatively simple and minimal practice is required, but it is worth spending a little time practising on scrap mount-board to get the technique right. The pen can be used in one of two ways; either by 'pulling' it towards you, which is probably the most natural way, or 'pushing' it away from you, which has the advantage that your hand does not mask the start and finish points on the mount.

The straight-edge should be as long as can be handled comfortably and must have a bevel on one edge. It is used with the bevel facing downwards, so that the pen will not be encouraged to bleed ink under the edge, thus spoiling the mount. The alternative is to use a bevelled-edge plastic ruler upside down.

Inks for drawing lines on board need to be chosen carefully. Although diluted watercolour can be used quite effectively on white and off-white boards, it is transparent and therefore cannot be used to draw light-coloured lines on dark-coloured board. Specially developed inks for mount decoration are available and it is advisable to use these inks wherever possible.

The secret to good ink lining is to avoid over-filling the pen, to work firmly and evenly, and to keep the pen as upright as you feel comfortable with. The best way to fill the pen is with a small brush, wiping off any excess before you rule the line.

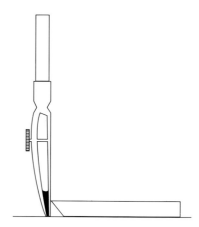

A marking pen should always be used against a straight-edge or a ruler with the bevel positioned face down to avoid ink bleeding under the edge.

Ink lining – step-by-step

1 A corner marking device, which fits into the 90° angle of the 'window' is used to mark out the lines.

2 Load the pen carefully and make a few practice lines before you start.

3 Rule the line firmly with a continuous even movement of the pen.

Washlining

Although much can be done in mount decoration with ink lines alone, the next progression is to the 'washline' mount: a wash, or pastel shade of colour, enclosed by ink lines. There are two methods of washlining – the traditional method using watercolours and the more modern method using powders – or you can stick down pre-prepared, self-adhesive, washlining paper.

Washlining using water colours

With the traditional method of washlining, you start by marking out the start and finish points for the ink lines on a prepared mount. For now, link these points together with a very faint pencil line. Equip yourself with watercolour paints, a palette, two appropriately sized brushes and a pot of clean water. Mix a dilution of the colour you intend to use and test it on a piece of scrap board. The effect should be very pale with just a hint of colour.

Take a clean brush and load it with clean water. Carefully 'paint' the area enclosed by the pencil lines with water, being very careful not to allow the water to bleed over the edge of the pencil lines. Make sure the panel is evenly damp, then immediately repeat the process with the colour wash using the other brush. Work both ways along the panel from the first corner, being careful not to allow any drying of the liquid. Keep both ends moving and wet until you reach the opposite corner and gently run the two ends together. Finish off by removing any pooling with a squeezed-out brush or a cotton bud.

The points to remember when using this method are:
• be as accurate as you can with the first covering with clean water as the colour will go wherever the water is;
• once started, do not stop;
• prevent 'pooling' of colour which will result in dark patches;
• finish off neatly.
When the washline is dry, draw in the ink lines. Use four or more lines for each panel. For the best results vary the depth of the colour of the ink by diluting with water. Finish off the outer lines with a darker colour.

Washlining – step-by-step

1 *With the ink lines marked lightly in pencil, fill in between them with water, applied with a clean brush.*

2 *Use a second brush to apply the diluted colour wash, avoiding 'pooling' at the corners.*

3 *When the wash is dry, draw in the ink lines using your ruling pen. Add more lines if required.*

Washlining using powder

An easier method of washlining is to buy a kit of powders that are specially made for the purpose. This method of applying the wash is completely dry, so the ink lines are drawn first. When these are dry, take the appropriately coloured powder and the special applicator that comes with the kit and apply the colour to the panel with a gentle rubbing action. Work reasonably neatly to the ink lines but do not worry about any 'scatter' as this will be removed later. When the panel is evenly coloured by the powder, take a wad of cotton wool and gently buff the panel so that the binding agent in the powder is allowed to work. Now place a straight-edge along the ink-line nearest to the panel. With the eraser provided, remove any excess powder that has escaped over the lines. You can leave off halfway through if necessary with this method as nothing will spoil.

Pre-prepared washlines

You can buy rolls of pre-prepared self-adhesive washlining paper (available in different widths) and simply stick this down on the mount, mitring it neatly at the corners. For a different effect, you could also use marbled paper, available in sheets which you can cut into strips.

Powder washlining – step-by-step

1 First draw in the ink lines and then, using the applicator provided, apply the powder between them.

2 Gently buff the coloured panels with cotton wool to 'bind' the colour.

3 Use a straight-edge and the eraser provided to remove excess powder outside the ink lines.

Pre-prepared washlines – step-by-step

1 Start by marking the position of the washline, using a corner gauge.

2 Peel off the backing strip and lay the washline along your pencil lines, overlapping it at the corners.

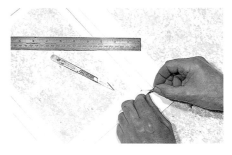

3 Cut through both thicknesses at the corner to give a neat mitre (remove the cut-off pieces).

Covering the mount with paper

There are many attractive marbled papers around, and these provide a simple but effective method of brightening up what can sometimes be an otherwise plain mount. Simply cut the mount-board to size and stick the marbled paper to it with PVA adhesive. Allow to dry and then mark out and cut the 'window' in the mount.

Covering a mount with wallpaper can produce an interesting effect and a wallpaper shop can be an Aladdin's Cave for mount decoration enthusiasts.

If you have followed the sponging method of decorating a frame, described on page 58, you could produce a 'mottled' mount to match the moulding exactly, either by using the same paper to cover the mount or by sponging directly on to the mount-board – do this before cutting the mount, as this will give a nice crisp white bevel.

Covering the mount with fabric

Linen, ready available from the haberdashery department of one of the big department stores, can be used for mount decoration and is particularly effective when used for covering the undermount when making a double mount, especially when framing anything with a

Covering the mount with paper – step-by-step

1   Coat the back of the paper with PVA adhesive.

2   Smooth the paper down over plain mountboard cut to size.

3   Cut the 'window' in the mount in the normal way.

nautical or ethnic flavour. Choose a fine weave and cut four strips about 25mm (1in) wide by whatever length is appropriate for the mount aperture. Take the undermount and lay face up on the bench. Mark a rough guide line about 12mm (½in) back from the bevel edge. Paint this area with PVA adhesive, being careful to paint the adhesive with a 'mitre' at each end.

Lay the first strip of linen on this area, lined up with the guide line, and press it firmly into place. Turn the mount over and lay it face down. Using a sharp blade, carefully cut the linen at either end along the adjacent bevel. Now paint a strip of adhesive along the underneath of the bevel roughly equivalent with the remaining width of the linen. Run your thumb along the bevel with the linen in between so as to score it and gradually work it around the bevel edge and on to the adhesive. Carefully press and pull away from the bevel so that the linen is tightly wrapped around the bevel. Turn the mount face up again. Take a small metal straight-edge and lay it across the mount from the corner of the bevel to the outside corner of the mount, and using a sharp blade, mitre the linen. Repeat this procedure with the other three sides and assemble the top mount to the undermount.

Covering the mount with fabric – step-by-step

1 To fit fabric to the undermount of a double mount, first cut the strips of fabric to size and then 'paint' PVA adhesive on to the front of the mount along one side.

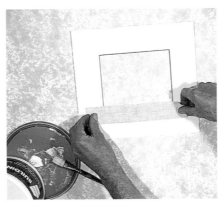

2 Lay the first strip of fabric over the adhesive and press it down.

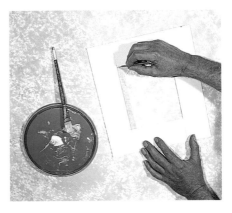

3 With the mount reversed, cut carefully along the side bevels.

4 'Paint' more PVA adhesive on to the back of the mount and press the line down, ensuring it fits tightly round the bevel.

5 From the front, 'mitre' the linen at the corners.

6 Repeat for the other three sides and assemble the double mount, exposing the fabric 'core'.

Covering the mount with suede

Probably the most attractive of all the cloth-based materials used in framing is something called 'display suede'; this something you might see on the walls of discos or hotel reception areas and is a thin material with a suede-like 'nap' on the surface, coming in a host of different colours. It looks particularly good when used in conjunction with flat gold slip and is perhaps most appropriately employed to impact an air of sumptuousness and luxury.

To use it on a mount, first cut the mount, using any piece of mount-board available, because the surface is of course going to be covered. At each corner, make a mark at 45° inwards toward the middle of the board, as far as possible. Now cut strips of the chosen suede about 6mm (¼in) wider than the mount borders are going to be. Apply PVA adhesive to one side of the mount, roughly to the width of the suede and work carefully to the marked 45° lines at either end. Lay a strip of suede along the edge leaving about 3mm (⅛in) of the edge showing. Press the suede firmly into the adhesive and ensure there are no wrinkles. Using a metal straight-edge and an artist's scalpel, cut the suede at the corners using the previously marked mitre lines as a guide. Run the cut the full length of the line as this will act as a guide for subsequent cuts. Repeat the process for the remaining sides, being particularly careful on the last corner as this is the only corner where you are working on top of the suede of the adjacent corner. When completed, turn the mount over and cut the aperture in the normal way.

To make the gold slip to go with the mount, subtract 10mm (⅜in) from the length and width of the aperture and mitre the slip to these sizes. The slip should fit under the mount showing the fluted edge plus 1 to 2mm of the flat, which is just about right. Use double-sided tape on the underside of the mount adjacent to the bevelled edge, to fix the slip in position. Make up the difference in level between the mount-board and the slip with 5mm foam-core board, as happily this is the same thickness as the slip.

The use of velvet as a covering material for mounts is illustrated in my *Framing a medal* project on page 92. Another useful material is hessian. Obtainable in various colours, it is useful for adding extra interest to unfinished slips. Simply cut into suitably sized strips and stick on to the flat surface of the slip before mitring.

Covering the mount with suede – step-by-step

1 Use a set square to mark 45° lines on the face of the mount-board and cut the suede into strips.

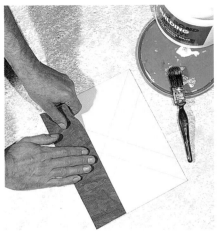

2 Stick down the first strip of suede along one edge after 'painting' this with PVA adhesive.

3 Mitre the corners of this strip, using a metal straight-edge and an artist's scalpel.

4 Repeat for the other side, taking great care when mitring the last corner.

5 The finished mount with the mitred gold slip in place.

Using paint effects

The advent of acrylic paints specifically designed for use with mount-board and moulding has opened up huge possibilities for decoration.

Many of the best styles of mount decoration are based on the double mount, using the undermount as the decorated component. As a start, try painting the 'garland of roses' effect.

Cut a double mount in the normal way, using perhaps a pale peach colour for the top mount. Paint the bevel and surrounding 12mm (½in) or so of the undermount with warm white acrylic paint. Prepare a diluted mix of clay red acrylic paint and take an old and suitably 'spiky' paint brush to stipple it all around the bevel randomly, showing the white base coat in between. Now prepare a similar mix in green and repeat this on top of the red, again allowing some of the base coat to show through. When the top mount is added you should have a very attractive effect of leaves and roses.

You could also hand paint your own designs on to the mount – for example, use the sponging technique described on page 58 to apply paint directly to the mount-board or use home-made or pre-bought stencils for special effects.

Stippling a double mount – step-by-step

1 Paint warm white acrylic paint around the bevel of the undermount.

2 Stipple dilute red paint on top of the white.

3 *Follow this by stippling dilute green paint, again allowing some of the base colour to show through.*

4 *When the double mount is assembled, the 'garland of roses' is exposed.*

Cutting glass

The glass for a picture frame needs to be exactly the same size as the mount – i.e. slightly smaller than the frame – so if you are having the glass cut for you, you can take along the completed frame (or the mount if it fits the frame) to get the size right.

The main drawbacks of cutting glass yourself are the space needed for storing the glass sheets, the disposal of waste (and broken) glass and the large working area needed for cutting even half sheets of glass.

However, it is helpful to know how to cut your own glass – in case you need to cut a larger piece down. All you need is a good glass cutter, a wooden T-square and a padded work area – perhaps a wooden board covered with carpet.

Carefully place the glass on to the padded area and put the T-square in position on the glass (with the cross-bar nearest to you) to the correct measurement, allowing clearance for the width of the glass cutter head, usually 2mm ($^3/_{16}$in). Hold the glass cutter like a pen, but with your second finger on the front edge of the cutter. Place the cutter at the top end of the glass, against the T-square edge, with the wheel just on the glass. Apply medium firm pressure and draw the cutter evenly towards you in one continuous stroke. Complete the cut by running off the edge of the glass on to the T-square head and then break the glass either by 'bending' it upwards at the cut or by pressing the cut down over a length of wood or the bench edge. When cutting off thin slivers, use flat-jawed glazier's pliers to 'snap' off the edge.

The technique of glass cutting takes one or two attempts to get absolutely right, but practice makes perfect. Always treat glass with respect, but never be afraid of it.

Once cut, clean the glass with a proprietary glass cleaner and place it over the subject, checking carefully for any stray bits of dirt. My own preference at this point is to tape all the way around the glass, fastening the glass, mount, picture and backing together as one unit. Apply the tape about 3mm ($^1/_8$in) on to the edge of the glass, smooth down firmly, and fold the rest neatly around the back. This makes for ease of handling but, more importantly, prevents any dirt or dust getting in under the glass when assembling into the frame.

If you are cutting your own glass, this should be done before the frame is made (the glass is the same size as the mount).

If you are having the glass cut for you, it is best to make the frame first – so the glass can be cut to suit the frame.

Cutting glass – step-by-step

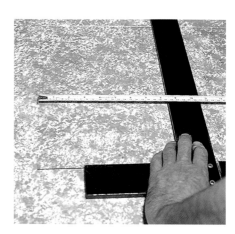

1 Position the T-square with its right-hand edge the correct distance from the edge of the glass.

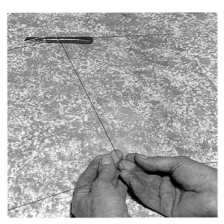

2 *Run the glass cutter firmly down the glass in one stroke, starting at the far edge.*

3 *You can usually break glass by pretending to 'bend' it upwards across the score line. If not, break it over a piece of wood on the bench.*

4 *To remove thin slivers of glass, use proper glass pliers to 'snap' them off at the edge.*

5 *Once the glass has been cut to size, it can be sealed to the mount, picture and backing as a 'sandwich'.*

Final assembly

When it comes to putting all the components together to make the whole picture frame assembly, cleanliness is essential – it is extremely annoying to turn the frame over after the final fitting of the picture wire, only to discover that there is a speck of dust under the glass and you have to dismantle everything and start all over again!

If you have not already made the 'sandwich' of glass, mount, picture and backing board described and illustrated on the previous page, do it now, remembering to clean the glass first and to be ultra careful to keep everything clean and straight.

The way you finish off the frame depends on how thick this 'sandwich' is. If, as usual, it is less than the depth of the rebate of the moulding, you can use glazier's 'darts' or panel pins to hold it in place, followed by taping or covering with brown paper.

Securing the picture in the frame

Place the 'sandwich' face up on the bench and make a final check for dirt or any other mishaps. Place the frame over it and then turn the complete unit over so that it is face down. Place your metal weight (or, for delicate frames, a padded block) against one side of the frame and fix the 'sandwich'

(glass/mount/picture/backing) in place with panel pins hammered in or a glazier's gun firing small triangular darts into the inner surface of the frame, flush against the backing. Apply one pin or glazing dart every 75 to 100mm (3 – 4in), holding the sandwich firmly into the frame. Put in more pins or darts if necessary.

A glazier's gun, firing triangular 'darts' is a quick and easy way to secure a picture in the frame.

When using panel pins (which takes longer), it is essential to support the outside of the frame.

Sealing the back

When the sandwich is firmly in place, the back should be sealed. This not only makes it look neat, but will keep out dust and moisture. The normal way of sealing the junction between the backing board and the moulding is to use tape.

Several different types of tape can be used for this, but avoid using masking tape as the adhesive can dry out in time and the tape will begin to lift and become unsightly. I find that the ordinary 'licky-sticky' gummed brown tape is the best choice as it is more easily formed around angles and shapes and also has a much better appearance, being a neutral buff colour, and is cheap!

An alternative method of sealing the frame, provided the backing board is level with or below the back surface of the moulding, is to cover the entire back with brown paper. There is a particular 'knack' to this, which makes the finished job as neat as can be. Cut a piece of brown wrapping paper slightly larger than the frame. Place the paper face down on the bench, dull side up, and dampen the back with a moistened sponge. While this is soaking, 'paint' the back of the moulding with PVA adhesive and then take the brown paper and smooth it, shiny side up, over the back of the frame. Make sure it is reasonably tightly stretched, and leave it to dry. As the paper dries, it will stretch itself drum-tight over the back of the frame and give an extremely neat finish. Trim off the excess.

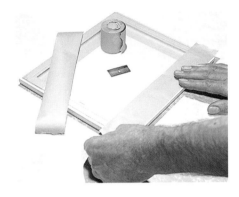

When using sticky tape to seal the back of the picture, position it squarely and make sure it is well tucked into the corners.

Brown paper covering the whole of the back of the picture gives a neater finish and can easily be trimmed to size.

Applying the fixings

The fixings for picture frame wire or cord are normally positioned around one-third the way down the sides of the frame.

To fit screw eyes, use a bradawl to make a pilot hole and then simply screw the eyes in by hand – if the wood is tough, use the bradawl as a turning device.

You should also use a bradawl for making pilot holes when fitting D-rings. These are screwed in place – choose screws of a material to match the D-rings (chromium plated or brass) so that there is no corrosion. The final task is to secure the picture hanging wire (or preferably nylon cord) between the screw eyes or D-rings. Tie the knot in the cord off centre, so that it will not interfere with the picture hook.

When using mirror plates (see page 40) to screw a picture permanently to the wall, use countersunk screws (brass if you are using brass mirror plates) and fit an appropriate wallplug in the hole in the wall.

A different method of fixing is used for pictures which are to stand on a table, a shelf or a chest. Here, you use a hinged strut, two-thirds the height of the picture, secured to the backing board. For details of this, see my *Photograph* project on page 84.

Fitting screw eyes.

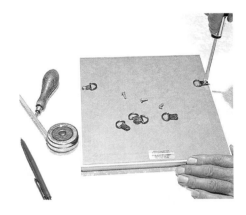

Fitting D-rings.

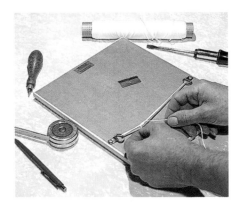

Fitting nylon picture hanging cord.

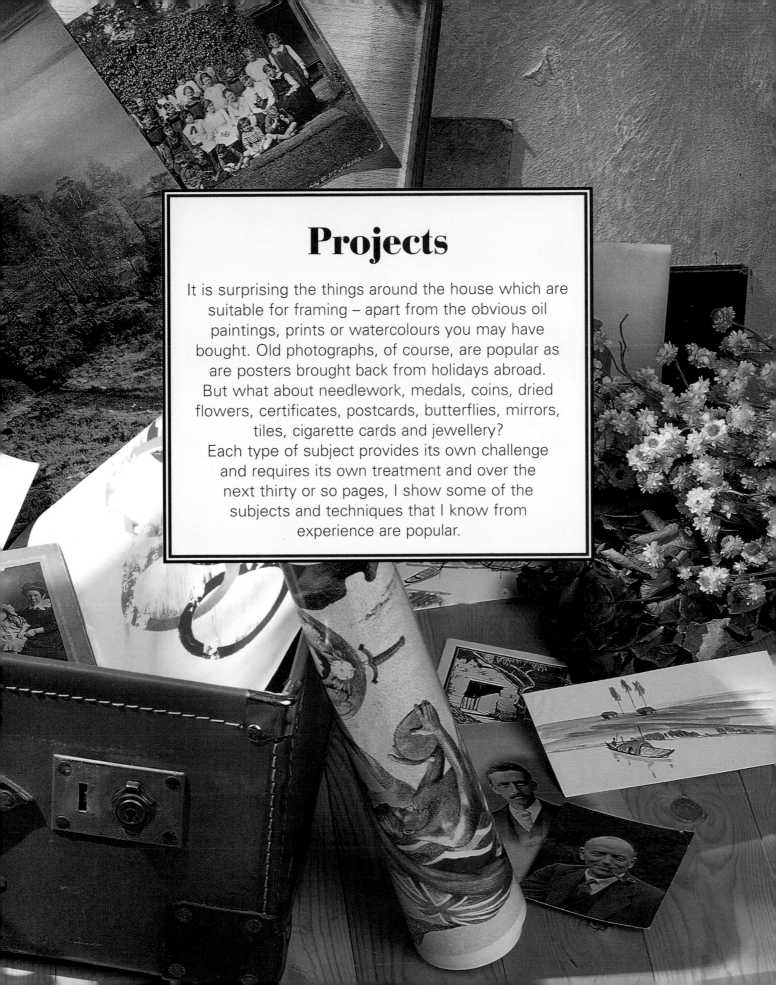

Projects

It is surprising the things around the house which are suitable for framing – apart from the obvious oil paintings, prints or watercolours you may have bought. Old photographs, of course, are popular as are posters brought back from holidays abroad. But what about needlework, medals, coins, dried flowers, certificates, postcards, butterflies, mirrors, tiles, cigarette cards and jewellery?
Each type of subject provides its own challenge and requires its own treatment and over the next thirty or so pages, I show some of the subjects and techniques that I know from experience are popular.

Project 1 **Photograph**

Framing an old black-and-white photograph is a regular job for most professional framers – so it is likely to be one of the first things an amateur wants to start on.

The subject needs to be treated sympathetically – where possible, try to use an oval mount as these are particularly suitable for a 'head and shoulders' shot or for a close-up of someone's face. The frame and the mount should be simple and tasteful – and draw the eye into the photograph.

Old black-and-white photographs generally look best in old or stained wood, which is very much in keeping with the period and 'sepia' or faded prints will look best with an off-white rather then a pure white mount. In short, the finished job should look as though it was still in its original frame.

For this old photograph, I have used an ivory mount-board with a gilded double oval mount and a mildly ornate patterned timber moulding about 20mm (¾in) wide which I have stained to give it a deeper colour.

Most photographs like this will stand on a table or chest rather than hang on the wall, so a 'strut back' has been fitted to the hardboard backing of the finished frame rather than picture wire.

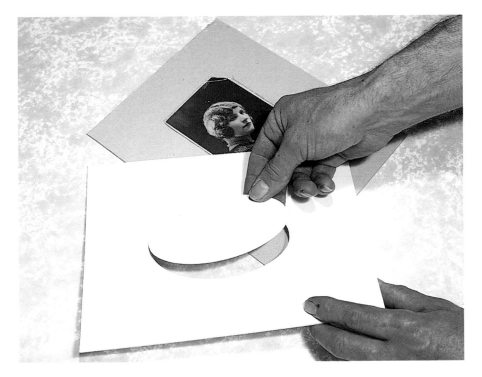

1 *The first step is to cut two pieces of mount-board to size and then to cut oval windows in each of them – the window in the upper (ivory) mount being slightly larger to allow the gilding to show through. Cutting ovals is not easy, but fortunately it is not difficult to buy mounts with the ovals already pre-cut.*

The undermount (which can be plain white) is primed and gilded using a proprietary gilding paint applied with a brush.

2 *Position the top mount over the undermount and stick them together using double-sided adhesive tape as close to the window as possible.*

3 *Position the double mount carefully over the photograph and 'hinge' the photograph in place using adhesive tape along the top of the photograph stuck to the back of the lower mount.*

4 *A 'strut back' is made up of a hinge clip, a hinge bar and a strut made from plywood, MDF or hardboard. The clip is fixed to the strut using 'bifurcated' rivets and the bar to the backing board by the same method. The strut then clips over the bar. You can buy complete strut backs made from black fibreboard or brown MDF; the alternative is to make up your own, either using MDF or hardboard ready-made struts (sometimes sold with the hinge clip already rivetted in place) or your own home-made plywood strut which can then be stained to match the frame moulding.*

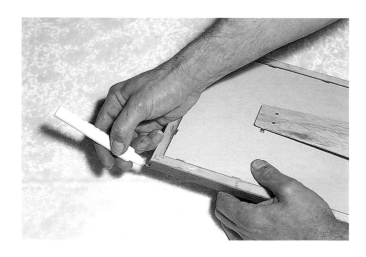

5 *The final job once the frame has been assembled is to go round the corners with a touch-up pen in case the stained moulding has chipped when it was being cut.*

Project 2 **Needlework**

Framing a needlework 'sampler' is another job I find myself doing a lot. Of varying standards of excellence, they are almost always of high sentimental value, but can also be some of the most difficult jobs to frame. What makes them tricky is where someone wants the frame to be close up to the needlework. Because the border then has to be stretched around the edge of the backing, the whole thing becomes very frustrating and time-consuming. It makes life a lot easier if you include a mount as I have done here – the material can then be fixed to the front of the backing, with the mount covering the fixing method (usually staples). Using a mount also keeps the material away from the glass and can enhance the subject.

For this project, commemorating a wedding, I have chosen a fairly narrow dark wooden frame with an inner gilded edge. This gilding is reflected by the use of a gold 'slip' fitted between the needlework and the mount. This is mitred at the corners in the same way as for making up a picture frame and fits underneath the bevelled 'window' in the mount.

The easiest way of fastening needlework in place is by stretching and stapling, using a staple gun. The staples will need firm board to fix to with sufficient thickness to absorb the length of the staple. A good combination for this is white mount-board over 6mm (¼in) foam-core board, which gives a good rigidity while remaining light in weight. The mount will cover up the staples.

1 Prepare a 'sandwich' of white mount-board and backing board with foam-core in the middle and staple the needlework to this with a staple gun stretching as you go – see Tips on Stretching Needlework *on page 90. Work with clean fingers as needlework is difficult to clean once it is stretched in place. Always use white board as a base as any other colour can show through the needlework.*

2 The gold slip is cut to a size to suit the needlework, mitring it at each corner and then a bevelled-edged 'window' is cut in the mount. Secure the slip to the mount using double-sided tape.

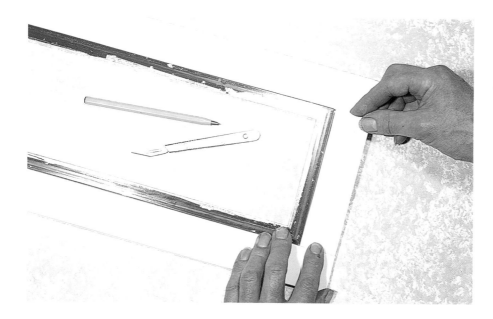

3 *Make up the difference between the back of the slip and the mount with scrap slips of foam-core. Add the mount to the work, trim to size and assemble in the frame – when making the frame, bear in mind that the combination of backing, needlework, mount and glass will be rather thick and it may be wise to go for a moulding with an extra high rebate where possible, so that the backing does not project above the frame at the back.*

Tips on Stretching Needlework

When you have prepared the backing board/foam-core/mount-board sandwich and laid the needlework on the surface, fix it in place in one corner with two staples, stretch and line up one edge parallel to the edge of the board, and secure again with two staples; don't over-stretch, light stretching should be sufficient.

Stretch one of the opposite corners and again secure in place, repeat this procedure with the last corner. While working, keep a check on any straight lines that may be present in the embroidery and keep them as straight as possible.

Now that the needlework is secured at all four corners, work along one edge applying staples as necessary and fix the edge in a straight line. Move to the opposite edge and work from the middle outwards stretching and stapling until the edge is as straight as possible. Repeat with the other two sides.

Some needlework or tapestries can come badly out of shape, almost diamond shaped rather than square. These are almost impossible to square up using the normal method and special treatment is required. Take a piece of stout plywood or similar and lay the subject on it face down. Secure with staples at one corner and stretch as square as possible. This can require brute strength so some help may be needed. When as square as can be, lightly dampen the piece with a spray of clean water and leave to dry. This usually results in the subject remaining square enough for normal stretching.

Extreme cases may require repetition of this treatment.

Project 3 **Medal**

Medals, medallions, plaques or coins or indeed any object that has any thickness to it, require special attention and can be some of the most interesting challenges in framing. This large medallion, commemorating a soldier from the First World War, is made of bronze and quite heavy and about 6mm (¼in) thick. It is to be mounted on brown velvet with a matching brown velvet mount.

In keeping with the subject, the 'window' in the mount will be circular and I have chosen black-core mount-board. A simple dark oak-coloured moulding is used to make the surrounding frame.

If you are framing a medal with a ribbon, it would be better to make a box frame as described in my *Dried Flowers* project on page 100. The ribbon should be stapled in place for additional security.

1   *The first step is to cut the mount-board to size and then to cover both it and a larger piece of backing board with the velvet, using PVA adhesive.*

2   *Then cut a circular window from the black-core mount-board around 12mm ($\frac{1}{2}$in) larger overall than the medallion. If you do not have an oval/circle mount cutter, hunt around for a circular object of the correct size to use as a template to guide your hand-held mount cutter.*

3   *Fix four pads of adhesive putty to the back of the medallion ...*

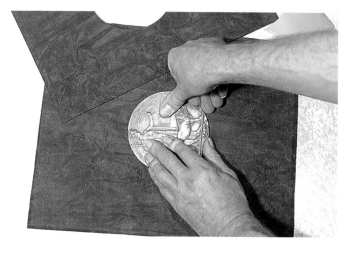

4 ... and press the medallion into place in the centre of the velvet-covered backing board (the exact positioning does not matter at this stage).

5 Because the medal is thicker than the (covered) mount-board, you will need to add spacing pieces of foam-core to the back of the mount to bring it level with the front surface of the medal.

6 Fix the mount exactly in place around the medallion using double-sided tape, trim the mountboard to size and make up the frame as normal.

Project 4 **Oil painting**

Oil paintings are in some ways some of the easiest of subjects to frame as they do not need mounts or glass. The actual stretching of the painting itself can present some problems to the new framer but, fortunately, made-to-measure, easy-to-use, stretcher bars are now readily available, which make life a lot easier. A word of caution about some of the paintings on canvas that you might buy on holiday abroad: these can have very narrow margins, which makes them difficult to stretch, so be careful to check before attempting framing.

Never use a narrow moulding on an oil painting; without fail, this never works and will simply result in a cheap-looking job. Even the smallest of oils need a substantial moulding to show them to their best advantage. Gilded frames, often with a highly ornate pattern, are the normal choice.

It is very easy to make an oil painting look crowded, so try and make use of 'slips' where possible as this gives the subject some space to 'breathe'. This is the approach I have used for this oil country scene, in effect making a frame within a frame.

1   *The first step is to assemble the stretcher bars with their mitres tight together. Hammer the stretcher wedges lightly into the corners.*

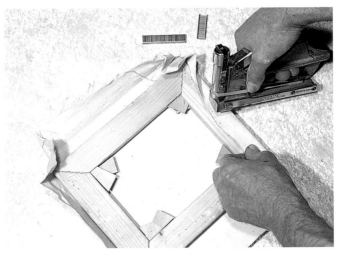

2   *Fix the canvas to the stretcher using a staple gun, pulling the canvas as taut as you can. Try to make the inevitable folds at the corners neat.*

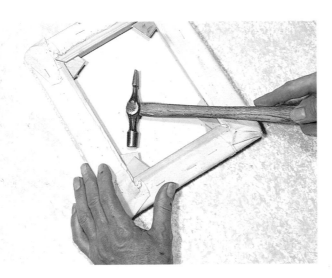

3   *Now hammer the stretching wedges home until the canvas is drum-tight.*

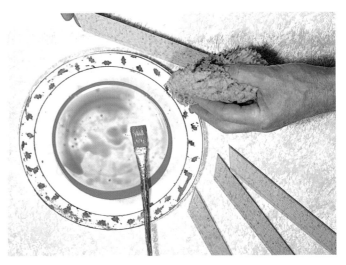

4   *It is best if the slip is given a decorative treatment which picks up the colours in the painting. For this picture, I have used a slip profile in unfinished obeche, first giving it a base coat of green-blue acrylic paint and then 'mottling' on a diluted coat of green acrylic paint, using a large natural sponge.*

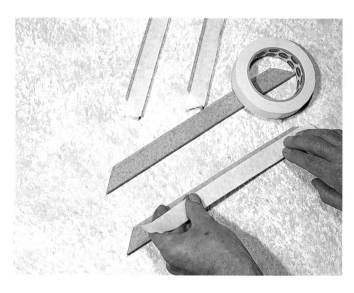

5 As only the 'sight-edge' of the slip is to be gilded, the next step is to mask the remainder, using ordinary masking tape, but pressing it down well.

6 A coat of gilt paint is applied with a small artist's brush.

7 Once the gilt paint is dry, peel off the masking tape carefully, join the four pieces of slip together at the corners and secure the slip to the stretcher with angled pins.

8 The ornate gilt frame is made up to suit the size of the slip and the painting/slip assembly is finally secured to the main frame by hammering more angled pins through the slip into the main frame.

Project 5 **Dried flowers**

Dried flowers, in common with other three-dimensional subjects, require special treatment to be displayed in a frame effectively. The best way is to arrange the flowers on a mount and then to put this into a 'box frame' about 25mm (1in) deep. The box can be made from foam-core and lined with an appropriately coloured mount-board – the advantage of using foam-core (rather than strips of timber) to make the box is that it can be any depth you want.

For this arrangement of dried flowers, I chose a moulding of a heavy proportion with a 'distressed' effect to enhance the natural effect of the subject; it also has a deeper than normal rebate to allow some chance of hiding the depth of the box. The box will, however, project from the back of the frame.

1 *The first step is to decide on the base area required for the box, then add on the depths of the sides. Cut a piece of foam-core to this size. Now mark the side depths on the foam-core, using a ball-point pen as pencil does not show up well on foam-core. On one side of each corner, say on both the long sides, mark the thickness of foam-core, which will be either 3 or 5mm (⅛ in or 3/16 in).*

2 *Score through the surface paper of the foam-core with a scalpel – do not cut all the way through. On the short sides, score a line all the way across at the side depth mark. On the two remaining sides, just score between the depth marks, not all the way across.*

3 *Now remove the corners. Cut right into the corners, but do not remove the thin pieces marked with the board thickness.*

4 *The edges may now be folded quite cleanly to assemble the box and the corners secured with white tape.*

5 *Place the arrangement of dried flowers on its backing mount in the box.*

6 *Now the box will need lining. Ordinary mount-board can be used but I have found that the new linen-covered boards now available are particularly effective for this – and this is what I have used for the base on which the flowers were mounted. Measure the depth of the inside sides. Cut four strips of the same board to this size. Working on two sides opposite to each other, cut two strips to length, and stick in place with double-sided tape, so that they hold the bottom piece in. Cut the remaining two sides to suit and fix in place.*

7 *Cut a narrow mount from the same mountboard and place over the box to hide the edge of the foam-core. Place the cleaned glass on top, make and add the frame and turn the whole assembly over after checking for any trapped dirt.*

8 *If, as is usual, the box is too deep for the rebate of the moulding a good way of fixing it to the frame is to use acrylic decorator's filler applied with a mastic gun. Allow to dry and neatly tape up.*

Project 6 **Watercolour**

The traditional way of treating a water colour is to use a washline mount, framed with a suitable high-quality gilt moulding. Some would say that this is the very epitome of picture framing. With most watercolours, which are usually delicate, you should use an off-white or ivory mount-board and match the colour of the wash to the most appealing colours in the painting. You will need the dry powder washline pigments, acrylic inks, a ruling pen, a bevelled straight-edge and a corner marking gauge (as described on page 68) for positioning the washline.

For this watercolour, showing a delightful country landscape, I have chosen a light green washline (to match the tree) with blue, green and brown ink lines and have surrounded the mount with a very expensive Italian gilt frame.

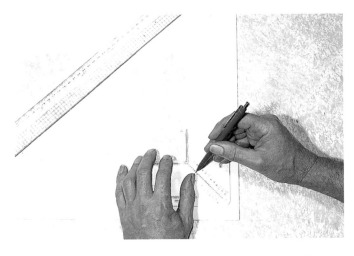

1   The first step is to cut the mount and mark the start and finish points for the ink lines, using the corner marking gauge.

2   Using the straight-edge with the bevel facing down, carefully draw the ink-lines. Work outwards from the bevel of the mount, completing one line all the way round at a time.

3   When the ink is dry, apply the appropriate powder liberally between the ink lines with the foam brush provided.

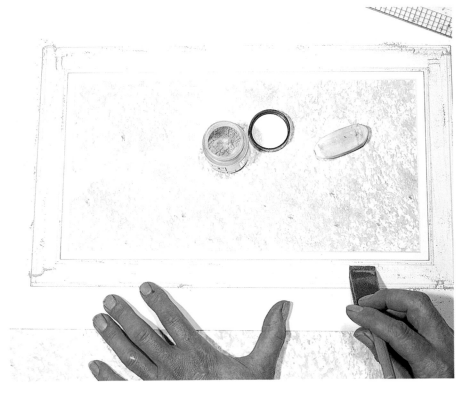

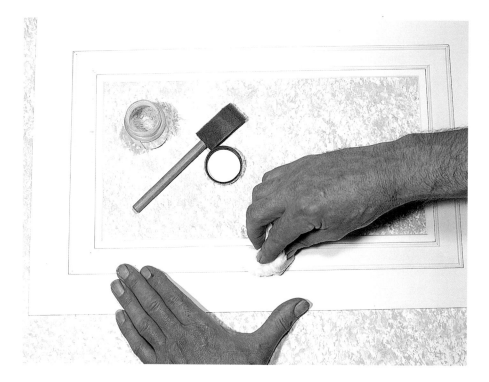

4 Blow away excess powder and buff gently with a wad of cotton wool.

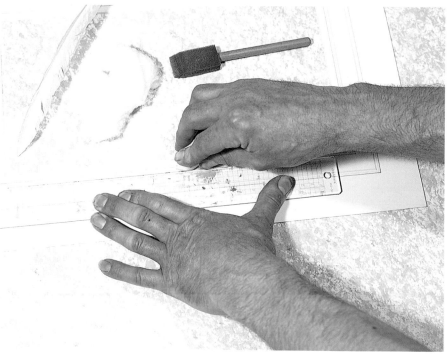

5 Lay a straight-edge on the inner ink-line and rub away any excess powder that may have escaped over the outside of the panel.

Project 7 **Family photo**

Family photos, by definition, usually come in multiples of at least three, and very pleasing groupings can be achieved. The normal approach to this kind of subject (and also to something like cigarette cards) is the multi-mount – several 'windows' cut in a single piece of mount-board.

This particular subject is a simple group consisting of Father, Son and Mother in that order from left to right and I went for a combination of rectangular and oval cut-outs, with the oval in the centre. For a more elaborate family gathering (family 'trees' are popular), circular cut-outs might be more appropriate.

Because the three original photographs were black-and-white (as is so often the case), an ivory-coloured mount-board was chosen for the upper mount with gilding showing through from the lower mount, but the combination of shapes and mount colours is endless and is limited only by your imagination (and your supplies!).

To frame the family photographs, I have chosen a plain 'spoon' moulding which is to be hand-decorated and waxed.

1   *The first step is to mark out the board and cut the windows in the upper mount – if you do not have an oval mount cutter, you could make the central window circular, using a suitably-shaped round object to guide your hand-held mount cutter.*

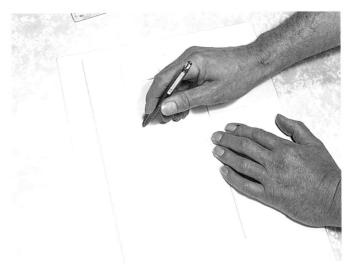

2   *With the windows cut in the upper mount, place this face down on the back of the lower mountboard and mark round the openings. Mark the width of bevel to be shown inside these marks, cut out the (smaller) windows in the lower mount and prime and gild the undermount.*

3   *Position the top mount carefully over the lower mount and secure them together using double-sided adhesive tape.*

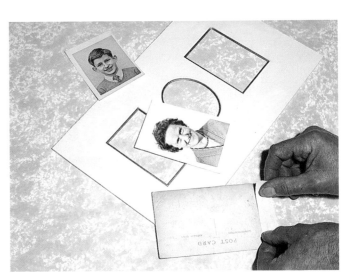

4   *Add the photos to the back of the lower mount by sticking them in place with tape.*

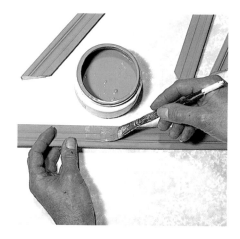

5 *Now you can start on the plain wooden moulding. First paint it with a base-coat of terracotta acrylic paint, using a wide brush.*

6 *When this base coat is dry, wash over with diluted dark brown paint and ...*

7 *... while still wet, rub over with a damp cloth to reveal the high spots of the moulding. Allow to dry.*

8 *To achieve the final effect, 'mottle' with a black/dark brown mixture and allow to dry.*

9 *Apply brushing-grade wax polish and allow this to dry.*

10 *Finally, buff the wax polish to a shine and assemble the frame.*

Project 8 **Poster**

We all have posters at home – perhaps a memento of a foreign holiday, a reproduction print or, as here, an old advertising sign.

Framing a poster is easy in one sense because you do not need a mount – but it can present a unique problem in that the best type of frame to show off a poster is often one of comparatively slim section. Because most posters are quite large, a standard timber moulding of this profile would be too weak to support the weight of the glass and backing.

This is where the excellent selection of aluminium extruded frames come into their own. They are slim in profile, but have great strength. They are generally supplied in mitred lengths, complete with all fittings for assembly and hanging; all you need to assemble them is a screwdriver.

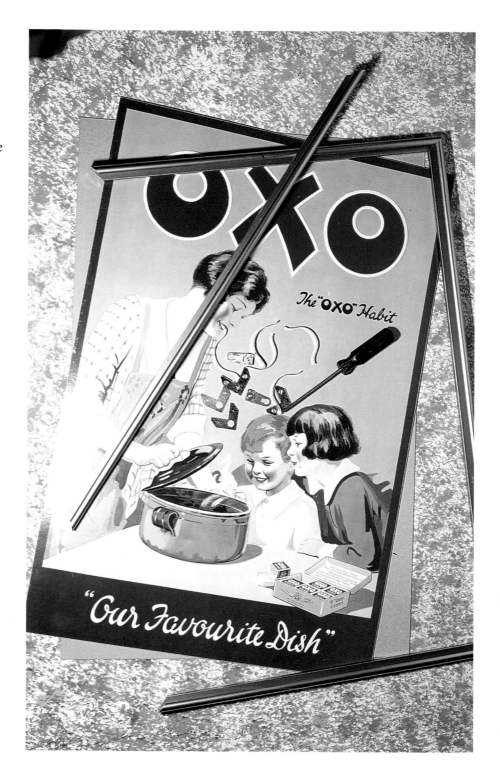

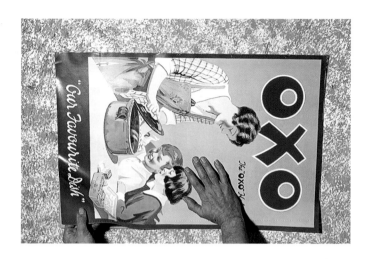

1 First of all, you need to stick the poster down on to an appropriate backing board cut to size and then cut the glass (or have it cut to size for you).

2 You can assemble three sides of the aluminium frame, using two of the special corner pieces supplied before sliding in the glass/poster/backing 'sandwich'.

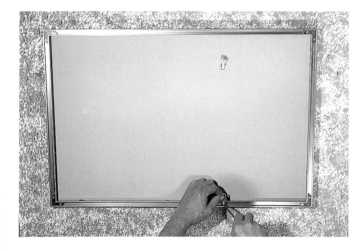

3 The final side of the frame is then screwed into place with two more corner pieces.

4 *Push in the springs supplied under the rebate of the aluminium extrusion to hold the backing and glass firmly in place.*

5 *Measure one third of the way down the frame and add the special hangers to take the picture wire or cord by screwing them in place.*

Hanging pictures

It is a good idea to think about where and how you are going to hang a picture when you are framing it. The style, size and decorations of the relevant room may well influence the choice of moulding and the mount (and how you decorate them) and the proposed method of hanging will obviously influence the fittings you attach to the back of the frame. Pictures are more than ornaments: they are an integral part of the decoration of your home. Positioned and lit correctly, they can enhance the decorative effect in different rooms; get this wrong and they can stick out like the proverbial 'sore thumb'.

Where to hang pictures

Some pictures, especially family photographs, you will want to have in frames to go on side tables, dressers, chests of drawers and the like. But everything else will go on the wall – and almost any spare wall space is a potential candidate.

Around fireplaces

A fireplace can look a bit bare on its own – but surrounded by pictures, it becomes a totally different object. A large single picture or mirror over the centre of the fireplace is traditional; in a larger room, you could perhaps surround this with smaller pictures on either side of the main picture, perhaps with extra ones low down either side of the fireplace itself.

Using a group of pictures above a fireplace is equally effective – perhaps linked with ornaments on the mantelshelf to give an integrated effect.

In halls

The hall is an ideal room for displaying pictures and can even become your own 'picture gallery'. The hall is the first room that visitors see when they visit your home and as they walk through it, what could be nicer than pictures to look at on the walls? Pictures here should be hung at eye level – and as it is a room through which people pass, you can be more daring in your choice of subject.

The hall is a good choice for a dramatic display of your boldest pictures.

This matching group of pictures balances the fireplace and echoes the small compartments within the fire surround.

Up the stairs

The wall beside a staircase also provides the possibility of having a display you can look at as you climb or descend the stairs. Ideally, the pictures should be thematically linked to one another and they should be hung in rising lines with the centre of each picture on a line following the slope of the staircase. You could use a bold subject on the wall which faces you when you climb or descend the stairs – so that you are walking towards it.

Living/dining rooms

You will probably want to display your finest pictures in the living room, but remember that you will most often be looking at them sitting down so they may need to be hung slightly lower than they are in the hall.

Think carefully about how the pictures are going to blend in with the furniture and soft furnishings and about how they will look from different angles.

In dining rooms, single large pictures are often best, but you should remember that the light will often be subdued (perhaps only candle light) so dark subjects should be avoided.

Follow the lines of a curving stairway for a balanced 'picture gallery' effect.

Bedrooms

You will want small intimate displays for a bedroom and delicate watercolours, flower prints and rural scenes work particularly well as do family photographs. Use the bedhead wall or the wall you see lying in bed for maximum effect.

Contemporary posters blend perfectly with the lightness of the furniture.

Bathrooms

There is no reason why you should not have pictures hanging in a bathroom (though you will need to be especially careful about sealing them thoroughly). Because of the steamy atmosphere, though, prints and reproductions are better choices than water colours, but above all you will want pictures that are restful to look at.

Kitchens

You have the same problem here as in a bathroom (steamy atmosphere), but the pictures you may want to choose should be bright and cheerful ones, perhaps with a 'cooking' theme – herbs, for example.

Old-fashioned prints and portraits suit both bedroom and bathroom.

Sophisticated and contemporary black-and-white prints echo the sleek black marble surface.

Pictures linked to furniture

There are several ways in which you can 'link' pictures to your furniture. Choosing matching wood moulding is one way, choosing pictures from the same era as the furniture is another and arranging the pictures on the wall to suit the size and shape of the furniture is yet a third.

Do not hang pictures too low over sofas (they could get in the way) and keep pictures within the overall width of the piece of 'matching' furniture. The ornaments used on top of furniture such as tables and chests should be considered, too – candlesticks and narrow vases, for example, tend to direct the eye upwards towards the pictures, while a table lamp may cast an interesting light over a picture. The size of the pictures should also be in sympathy with the size of ornaments – especially where you have things like small wooden boxes or silver-backed hairbrushes on display.

How to arrange pictures

A traditional group of four flower pictures enhanced by the real thing.

This large group of pictures has a continuity of theme and colour.

A single picture imaginatively framed can be a focus of attention.

Single pictures

A picture on its own can be used as the focal point of a wall or even a room, or it can be made to blend if it is framed in a 'sympathetic' way. Single pictures over furniture will link the seating area with the wall while a picture in an alcove will tend to emphasise what could otherwise be a forgotten area.

Small groups

Often you will have two, three or four pictures with a linked theme,

which you will want to hang together in a group. The obvious way of linking a group is to frame them in the same way – the same size, with the same moulding and the same mount – but even using the same colour of mount-board on two different subjects will help to link them together.

Often, arranging a group in a symmetrical pattern will be the most appropriate, but think about having them in a rising line or even on adjacent walls.

Large groups

Again, there should be some kind of constant theme running through

a group of pictures hung together – the group should be hung fairly closely together to make a whole; they do not all need to be the same size as long as they are cleverly arranged on the wall with no large voids.

Spacing pictures

When hanging pictures in groups you need to think carefully about the height you hang them on the wall and the spacing between them.

There is no substitute for trial-and-error for this – although you may be able to 'compose' a group by laying it out on the floor, you cannot see how pictures will look on a wall without having a helper hold them against the wall and then looking at them from different aspects until you are happy.

When carrying out your 'dry run', think about how the pictures will be lit at different times – will they reflect the light from a window during the day or from a lamp at night? If reflection is going to be a problem, you could consider using non-reflective glass, but read what I have to say about this on page 39 first.

Height above floor level is a critical point to consider when hanging pictures. For most pictures, eye-level is ideal and no lower than chest height, but in rooms where you both sit and stand, you may want to hang pictures between standing eye level and sitting eye level.

Single pictures can be positioned to match a feature of the room or a piece of furniture, but you need to take more care when positioning and spacing groups, especially when they are thematically linked.

Ways of spacing pictures

There are lots of different ways in which you can arrange pictures in groups.

In a grid This suits small pictures of the same size and shape, but you may need to make the horizontal gaps slightly smaller than the vertical ones to make the grid look symmetrical.

Like crazy paving This method of arranging is suitable where you have different sizes and is exactly like laying a crazy paving path – large pictures around the outside to create the overall shape with smaller pictures filling in the spaces in the middle.

In rows Something needs to line up when you arrange pictures in a single row. This can be either:
• the **tops** of all the pictures
• the **bottoms** of all the pictures or
• the **middles** of all the pictures.

If you have a double row, you could combine two methods at the same time, with one row lined up at the top and the other at the bottom.

Around a point If you imagine a single point on the wall, with vertical and horizontal lines running through it, you can arrange your pictures so that they sit symmetrically within the cross formed with the large pictures nearest the focal point and the smaller ones further away.

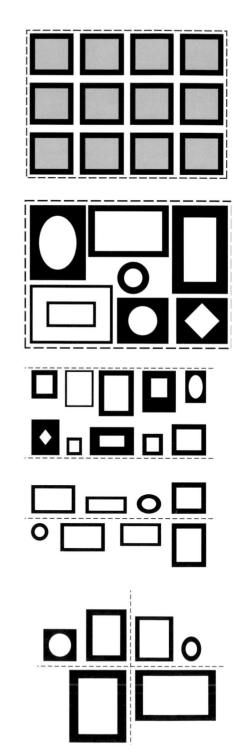

Lighting pictures

During the day, you will not normally need any artificial aid to lighting a picture – but it is not always a good idea to have a picture in strong sunlight. For a start, you may get unwanted reflections on the glass (especially if the picture is opposite a window), but more importantly the light can cause colours to fade and may also fade the wall surface around the picture leaving an obvious mark when the picture is removed. So keep delicate pictures out of direct sunlight.

The traditional way to light a picture after dark is with a picture light – a small brass light hooked over the top of the frame. This should not give any reflection provided the top of the picture is slightly out from the wall and is particularly appropriate with 'classical' pictures, especially

The recessed lights in the ceiling 'wash' these otherwise stark pictures with gentle light.

those in gilt frames. You should be careful with oil paintings however – too much heat can damage the glaze.

There are, however, many other ways of lighting pictures and you could consider uplighters positioned on the floor throwing light up to the picture, lamps positioned to shine light directly at the pictures or downlighters positioned in the ceiling throwing the light downward. Particularly effective are downlighters known as 'wall washers' which produce an overall light rather than a concentrated beam and you can have very unobtrusive low-voltage spotlights recessed into the ceiling or fitted to a track which produce a cool and concentrated light.

As with hanging pictures, there is no substitute for trial and error

A traditional brass picture light, mounted on the brass rail from which the picture is hung.

Free-standing lights provide dramatic lighting for the pictures.

when it comes to lighting, trying out different methods at different times of the day, before you decide on the final solution.

The practicalities

In Victorian homes, the standard method of hanging pictures was by special hooks from a picture rail – a wooden moulding or a brass rail fitted high up on the wall.

This method can still be used (assuming you have or can fix a picture rail) but most pictures these days will be fixed to the wall by some kind of hook or other suspension system secured directly to the wall itself.

Weight is a strong influencing factor when considering a method of hanging. A good basic rule is that any frame weighing over 4.5 kg (10 lb) is too much for a hammered-in picture hook and at this point drilling and plugging the wall to take a screw should be the safest solution. Also, pay close attention to the type of material

Traditional moulded picture rail supporting pictures.

used for the actual cord on the picture itself. Polyester cord is ideal for the lighter uses; wire and chain for heavier subjects.

When choosing wire, it is advisable to go for the soft stainless steel type which is easily twisted and wrapped, but is corrosion free, and will leave no stains on walls. It is available in several different strengths from 9 to 27 kg support weight. Chain is the strongest support but can be unsightly and is used only for ultra-heavy pieces where safety is more of concern than appearance.

How many hooks?

For most pictures a single wall hook is adequate, but on longer landscape-format pictures, two hanging points should be provided in order to give the stability necessary to stop the picture 'dipping' to one side. Another aid to this is to use small 'bumpers' on the bottom corners of the frame. These are small self-adhesive pads of foam or plastic which also

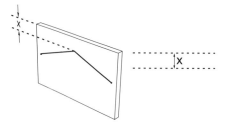

Transfer the measurement 'X' from the picture to the wall.

protect the wall surface from marking and provide a gap behind the picture which allows air to circulate and prevents mildew forming on the wall.

Exactly where to position the hanging point on the wall can often be a 'hit and miss' exercise, so a simple formula is worth adopting. Once you have decided where the top edge of the frame is to be, lightly mark this on the wall. Now pick the picture up by its hanging cord in the middle, allowing the full weight of the picture to hang from it, and measure the distance from where the cord passes over your finger to the top edge of the frame. Mark this distance below the line on the wall and fix the hook at this point, centrally for one hook or around a quarter the width of the picture in from either side for two. When arranging pictures horizontally, take half the width of each picture and add the required space between them; this is the distance for the hooks.

Using picture rails

In some homes (especially older ones), it is necessary to be able to hang pictures without damaging the wall in any way – for instance, on fabric-covered walls, panelled walls or on ornate plasterwork. Here, it is necessary to use a hanging system based on the picture rail – something you also may want to do where the wall is only lath-and-plaster or plasterboard which will give little support to a picture hook.

Where a picture rail is already in position, so much the better. If not, it will be necessary to provide one, nailed or (preferably) screwed to the wall. Different types of picture rail are available and there will be a good choice at local timber merchants.

The traditional way of hanging pictures from a rail is to use long lengths of wire or cord, attached to a metal hook positioned over the rail. But there are many other ways of using a picture rail, including ribbons and rope, and one of my favourites (and the one of the most unobtrusive) is to use Perlon suspenders, available from specialist framing suppliers. Perlon is a translucent plastic 'wire' almost invisible but very strong. Once the picture rail is in place on the wall, a special hook to suit the rail is fixed to the end of an appropriate length of Perlon. Additional adjustable fittings are then added to the length of Perlon from which the pictures will hang; these are adjustable for height and lock in place wherever necessary by means of a built-in screw clamp. The advantage of this system is that pictures can be 'stacked' one above the other as required and

adjusted to suit. No fixings into the wall surface are needed and pictures can be moved as you like.

Using picture hooks

Picture hanging pins and hooks are widely available and are normally secured directly to the wall surface with hardened pins which will not bend as they are hammered home. Hooks come in both single and double versions; double ones have two pins for greater security.

You can also get hooks designed for use where very hard surfaces

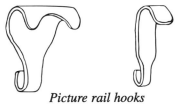

Picture rail hooks

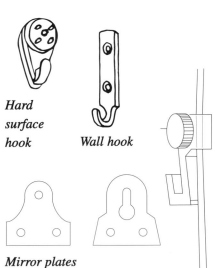

Hard surface hook   *Wall hook*

Mirror plates

Perlon hook

are encountered, such as brick or concrete etc. The hook itself is moulded plastic and has four short, very hard, pins built into it. The hook is simply put in place on the wall and the pins hammered home.

Other methods of hanging

Where a heavy picture has been fitted with 'mirror' plates, these are secured directly to the wall using screws into wall plugs. Another choice is to have two wall hooks to the wall which fit into slotted mirror plates on the back of the picture.

If you want to make your picture hanging method more interesting, you could add some decoration. Normally, this means concealing the hanging cord or chain with a relatively ornate bow or swag made from attractive ribbon or cloth, but sometimes decorative fabric can also be added to the top or side.

These imaginative treatments show just some of the ways in which you can add interest to the picture hanging method.

Buying picture framing goods

Many of the tools, equipment and materials you might need for picture framing can be bought readily from existing shops – many art shops, for example, will sell inks, paints and mount-board including ready-cut mounts (and some may sell small ready-made frames for you to decorate), while do-it-yourself shops will sell many of the tools you need (including mitre saws) and some may have a range of mouldings.

But for a wider selection of picture frame moulding and mount-board and for some of the more specialised tools, materials and equipment, you will need to go to a specialist picture framing supplier.

Some of these will be in the telephone directory, but will all be mixed up with professional framers (who will expect to do the job for you), so you need to find out which local firms you can do business with. An evening-class picture-framing tutor may be able to point you in the right direction.

You may even be able to come to an arrangement with a local framer – for example, if you need an oval mount to be cut or a frame made from a particular delicate material which you might make a mess of.

Most framers will be happy to do whichever part of the job you want and many may be prepared to sell you small amounts of moulding or things like picture wire, fixings and fittings.

The firms listed here are mostly wholesale firms who supply professional framers. But most will deal with amateur picture framers – and, if you spend enough money with them (some have a minimum order), firms like these will be happy for you to open an account and then to deliver the goods to you (an important consideration when you are buying whole lengths of moulding or even half sheets of glass!).

You may also be able to buy picture framing goods by mail order from firms who specialise in supplying the home picture framer – this has the advantage that you can usually buy in smaller quantities, though you will often have to pay a little more per item.

Some moulding suppliers operate a 'chop' service, where the moulding is sold already cut to size (with 'professional' mitres) for you to join together. So you do not have to find room for storing loads of moulding which may take you years to use up.

Alla Hardisty Supplies, Glen Arran, Stokesley Road, Northallerton, North Yorkshire DL6 2UD   01609 777670

Attic Framing Supplies, Unit 11, Boulton Industrial Centre, Icknield Street, Hockley, Birmingham, West Midlands B18 5AU   0121 551 5454

Berlyne Supplies, PO Box 1, Fielding Street, Middleton, Manchester M24 6BS   0161 653 7878

Charisma Picture Framing, 57–59 Station Road, Harrow, Middlesex HA1 2TY   0181 863 7614

Edward Henry Ltd., 21 Pitcliffe Way, Upper Castle Street, Bradford BD5 7SG   01274 737366

Homeframe Supplies, PO Box 191, Redhill, Surrey RH1 6FW   0181 760 9989   (Mail Order)

Lion Picture Framing Supplies, 148 Garrison Street, Bordesley, Birmingham B9 4BN   0121 773 1230

Mastermount Products, Alderley Road, Chelford, Cheshire SK11 9AP   01625 860850

Merseyside Framing Arts, 62–64 Wavertree Road, Liverpool L7 1PH   0151 708 5121

Origin Framing Supplies, Ridges Yard, 107 Waddon New Road, Croydon, Surrey CR0 4JE   0181 686 7462

Wessex Pictures, Unit 5, 2–4 Paisley Road, West Southbourne, Bournemouth BH6 5ET   01202 433070

Wessex Pictures (Ashford), Units 2 & 3, Hilton Business Centre, Kings North Industrial Estate, Wotton Road, Ashford, Kent TM23 2LL   01233 637104

Index

Acknowledgements

The author and the publisher gratefully acknowledge the help of the following in the production of this book:
Origin Framing Supplies, for allowing us to use their framing classroom to take pictures in and for providing various products and materials
Record Holdings for the corner clamp photograph used on page 28
Krystyn Holloway for her invaluable work on putting together the Picture 'gallery'
Gilt Edge Picture Framing of London SW6 (0171-731 7703) for providing pictures for use in the Picture 'gallery'
Photography on pages 8 & 9 by Paul Ryan/International Interiors.
Elizabeth Whiting & Associates supplied transparencies on pages 118 (bottom left) & 120 (left) by Mike Crockett, pages 118 (bottom right), 119 (top) & 123 (bottom left) by Michael Dunne, page 119 (bottom) by Spike Powell, page 121 (bottom right) by Debi Treloar, and page 123 (bottom right) by Neil Lorimer.
Photography on pages 120 (top right) & 121 (top right) by Simon Brown/The Interior World Picture Library.
Photography on pages 121 (left), 123 (top) by Julie Phipps/Arcaid.
Photography on page 124 by Ian Parry/Abode.
Photography on page 125 by Simon Lee/Homes & Gardens/Robert Harding Syndication.